SIN C

adventures of

C000083820

'From his inauspicious start as ~~Kelvin MacKenzie's News~~ Bunny at L!VE TV to his world tour as presenter of Bravo's *Sin Cities*, Hames manages to capture the rock 'n' roll decadence of gonzo television-making at its rawest, most visceral and dangerous. Whether he's having his scrotum pierced in Paris, being potentially buggered in Nice, arrested for drugs in Sweden, or overdosing in Buenos Aires, Hames charts his frequently-hilarious and harrowing adventures with humour, humility and at times, brutal honesty. His writing gives a unique insight into the heart of darkness that beats within all great documentary makers. Irresponsible, insane but inspired, the Queen should present Ashley Hames with a knighthood and a straightjacket as this fine book amply illustrates that he is equally deserving of both.'
Piers Hernu, *journalist and broadcaster* '

Ashley Hames has approached literature with the same courage and candour that he brought to his investigations of porn stars, perverts and prostitutes. The result is a picaresque tale brimming with hilarious encounters and moments of deep moral shame, all recounted with the nothing-to-lose honesty of a man confessing his sins to a priest on his death bed. Book fans will also be pleased to note that *Sin Cities* contains more hot-fisting and crazy lezbo action than *Bleak House* and *Tess of the D'Urbervilles* put together.'
Grub Smith, *journalist and TV presenter*

'There's something endearing about a man who uses the phrase 'front bottom' despite having had his balls nailed to a plank of wood, a bottle of red wine poured up his jacksie and numerous nights of passion with porn stars, prostitutes and a Playboy Bunny. Honest, funny and open-minded towards all manner of kink, Hames makes you think about what 'normal' really is – and consider how far you'd be prepared to push your own limits.'
Emily Dubberley, *founding editor, Scarlet magazine*

'A completely honest and candid description that cuts through stereotypical views of the adult entertainment industry, presented with factual 'hands on' experience rather than rumour. I simply love this book!'
Taylor Wane, *porn star*

'Sex, drugs and, er... some more sex. An unashamedly candid, funny, jaw-dropping and surprisingly reflective account of one man's adventures on the outskirts of perceived normality. And he seemed such a nice boy.'
Angela Ferrara, *editor, Deep-London magazine*

'A pile of shit.'
Kelvin MacKenzie, *former newspaper editor*

Ashley Hames is a television presenter, renowned as the face of Bravo TV's highest-rating television show, *Sin Cities*. Featuring 'everything adult', the programme attracted critical acclaim, as Hames investigated such topics as first-time porn actresses, adult babies, S&M culture, tentacle porn and self-abuse along with other bizarre sexual fetishes. In another Bravo favourite, *Man's Work*, he worked in some of the world's most demanding jobs — including anti-narcotics enforcement and crime scene cleaning. Known for his no-holds-barred approach to presenting and a curiosity for the absurd, Ashley is regularly seen on TV around the world and continues to make interesting and thought-provoking TV for a growing audience of fans.

www.thesexreporter.tv
www.myspace.com/ashleyhames

SIN CITIES
adventures of a sex reporter

ASHLEY HAMES

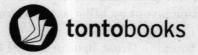 tontobooks

www.tontobooks.com

Published in the UK in 2008 by Tonto Books Limited
Copyright © Ashley Hames 2008
All rights reserved
The moral rights of the author have been asserted

The names of some people in this book have been
changed to protect their employment prospects

ISBN-13:
9780955632600

British Library Cataloguing in Publication Data:
A catalogue record for this book is available from
the British Library

Cover photograph by James Stafford
Photo section layout by Elliot at www.preamptive.com

Printed & bound in Great Britain by CPI Cox & Wyman

Tonto Books Ltd
Newcastle upon Tyne
United Kingdom

www.tontobooks.com

For Jon Sullivan and Las Vegas.

contents

contents

a note from the author

Oddly, until I became the host of *Sin Cities*, sex had never played a hugely significant role in my life; but after several years on the road visiting hundreds of cities across the world, I have pretty much seen and done everything there is to know about sexual fetishes, porn and the adult industry.

As one of those lucky few, I thought that by sharing my experiences, I could help give a few pointers to the more curious amongst you. And if you're not dissuaded from indulging in some of the naughtier sides to life, well, then I can lie back and think that at least I helped some of you find what you might be looking for.

More than anything else, I'm amazed that I ended up on such intimate terms with adult entertainment. In the pre-internet years and living life as a slightly fey, middle-class teenager, the closest contact I ever had with the more risqué side of life was through the occasional well-worn porno mag or, rarer still, a bog standard porn video. Back then, the sex industry was an unreal, abstract and untouchable place, full of rebellious creatures living very different lives to my own. But before too long, the English public schoolboy that I was had become a seasoned veteran of hundreds of porn shoots, S&M clubs, swingers' parties, fetish nights, orgies and gang bangs.

So how then, did I become known as the 'Prince of Porn' and 'Pornoman' and be able to boast, as one viewer kindly told me, of having 'Britain's Best-Known Penis'? Was it all down to a lucky break... right time, right place... talent..? Well, for me what started out as a fun job in the low-rent television industry took me on the most bizarre journey of a lifetime, as far away from reality as I could ever have imagined... a journey that I'm taking you on now.

prologue

'Just remember, Ashley, this is only television. People watch it and then they forget about it. You don't have to get hurt in the process of actually making it. Take care and look after yourself a bit more.'

If only I'd listened. Just a few months after hearing this advice, the cameras were rolling as I lay on an operating table in the medical room of a Parisian knocking shop. Looking down at me was Mistress Elsa, a specialist in cock and ball torture. In one of her hands was a hammer, in the other a nail. She pulled out a piece of wood that was solid except for a small hole cut in the centre, and placed it on top of me. Then, with practised skill, she took hold of my bollock-bag and pulled it gently through the hole.

'What we shall do is stretch out the scrotum and then I will nail it into the wood. It will be very pretty.' She smiledand licked her lips in anticipation.

Christ! This was going to hurt so fucking bad. 'OK, OK, come on then. Go for it.' I was ready. I was psyched. I was shaking like fuck and wanted to be anywhere other than here. And I wanted to not be broadcast on television while it all happened. Mistress Elsa took hold of may nuts and stretched my ball-bag out like a canvas. She then placed the tip of the nail on top of the skin. I screamed. Loudly.

Now imagine the sound I made as she drew the hammer back, ready to knock it through. All in a day's work, as they say. I have no idea who 'they' are, but they obviously never had the pleasure of working on *Sin Cities*.

chapter 1
a big red ferrari and
a shambling shit-tip

My story starts in 1995 when I applied for a job as a researcher in television. At the time I was earning my crust as a 'serious' radio journalist – researching, writing and broadcasting hard news stories. It was all a little bit too earnest for my liking. Somehow it didn't match my lifestyle, which, at the time, was going out, getting drunk and trying to get laid. Repeat. And then do it again at the weekend. All of which wasn't ideal for grinding out a living behind a news desk. Whereas television... well, television spelled out glamour, parties, money, action, and girls. Fortunately I was to find out all the rumours were entirely true: brilliant.

I arrived for my interview which, as it turns out, was at L!VE TV – then a struggling cable TV station based in Canary Wharf, East London. It was known at the time for two things: *Topless Darts* and extremely low viewing figures. *Topless Darts*, featuring girls in G-strings (and nothing else) playing semi-competitive darts, had garnered some rare publicity for the channel, giving it a reputation for smut and sensationalism.

Janet Street-Porter had set the station up with the backing of Mirror Group Newspapers but had left amid much controversy and an infamous BBC documentary, *Nightmare on Canary Wharf* – which pretty much summed up the station's fortunes at the time.

As I made my way up to Canary Wharf for my job interview, I was a twenty-six year-old lad thinking, well, not much really. At the time, I had no idea what L!VE TV was all about: I'd never heard of it before, never watched it, and hadn't been arsed to do any research in preparation. It dawned on me that complete ignorance coupled with the usual hangover probably wasn't the ideal interview technique as I tentatively entered the office of the Director of Programmes, and now LBC Radio broadcaster and Richard and Judy rent-a-gob, Nick Ferrari. The former Sun showbiz columnist was also famed for a fiery temper and a hefty gut. If I wasn't so fragile and lethargic, it would have been easy to get intimidated by the situation.

Nick began the interview by peppering me with questions about what type of newspaper I liked (The Independent, The Guardian), what news programmes I watched (*BBC News*, *Newsnight*) and what kind of interests I had (er... going out?). All of my replies gave him a pretty good idea of the type of person I was at the time – a slightly confused, laid-back, scruffy, left-wing, middle-class waster. In other words, I was someone completely unsuited to working in a highly energised, racy, tabloid-oriented television station.

'For fuck's sake,' he barked. 'You stroll in here with your silver spoon still hanging from your mouth; you read

The Independent and watch the BBC. You obviously have no idea what this place is all about.' The aggressive and confrontational Ferrari didn't mince his words.

'What's wrong with The Independent? That's where you advertised the job.'

As a comeback, it wasn't too shoddy. Ferrari glared at me.

'OK sunshine, what do you know about the Fred and Rose West case?'

Long pause. I was struggling to think straight. The Wests had recently been arrested and charged with the murder of a number of drifters who had camped out at their Gloucester home.

'Nothing really,' I replied, 'but I can tell you a joke about it.'

'Go on then.'

'What's Fred West's favourite drink?'

No reaction. Ferrari continues to stare at me.

'Tennents.'

A smirk crept its way across Ferrari's flushed face.

'OK mister, that's what you're going to be working on. Starting Monday, you're researching a documentary about the Wests. Come and have a look around.'

As job interviews go, it was one I'll never forget. And bizarrely, that was it – interview over. I had got the job and, sure enough, the following week I started my new job in television.

L!VE TV took up the entire 24th floor of London's Canary Wharf tower. A self-contained broadcasting entity, it was fully equipped with studios, gallery, editing suites, and transmission room. It was the perfect place for a young chancer like me to learn the entire process of making television from start to finish. All the shows were made in-house and, as briefed, I began work on a programme about Fred and Rose West. After just a few weeks, my time there was extended and I was hauled in to help out on another couple of documentaries. I had been doing pretty well and was happy there. It was full of young, thrusting media types, some with the talent to match their ambitions, others who were completely useless but talked the talk and somehow slipped beneath the radar of their superiors. This is a trend that I've since discovered is endemic in the television industry. There's a lot to learn in TV, and some people don't seem to get beyond the first couple of steps on that learning curve, but still manage to bullshit their way through the system and enjoy lucrative careers – they know the right people, say the right thing at the right time, or pass the buck for their mistakes onto other people below them in the food chain. As the saying goes – how many people work in television? About ten percent of them.

In the first few months of being there, I was enjoying it more than anything I had ever done before. Making television, although sometimes extremely difficult and frustrating – especially on the ultra-low budgets on which we operated – just didn't seem like graft to me. That's hard to explain. I've sometimes heard musicians speaking about the fact that they feel they have music inside them and have to get it out of their system regardless of whether it sells to an audience or not. I somehow felt the same about television. Very quickly I felt like I'd found my calling. Television was part of me, whether I liked it or not. Fortunately, I loved it and loved being part of it.

At the time, L!VE TV was an exciting place to be. Since Street-Porter's departure, legendary former Sun editor Kelvin MacKenzie had been brought in to knock the place into shape. His mandate was to increase viewing figures which had dipped to levels so low they scarcely registered. With audience figures directly linked to advertising revenue, the popular touch of Kelvin was seen as vital to the survival of the station.

His solution was a simple one – to put more stuff on the box that blokes liked; namely tits and football. At that time in the mid 90s, 'lads mags' epitomised by Loaded, FHM and Front magazine were all the rage. In football, the Premiership had just replaced the old first division and footballers were the new rock stars. Kelvin's Big Idea was to get Page 3 girls fronting programmes about football, thus killing two birds with one stone. It all made perfect sense. Well, sort of.

I remember the day Scottish glamour girl Kirsten Imrie stepped in to replace another former Page 3 girl, Gail McKenna, as the presenter of the channel's bargain basement version of *Match of the Day*, called *Sport Night Live*. The producers were tearing their hair out at the fact that Kirsten could scarcely focus her eyes let alone read an auto-cue. Kirsten was a sweet girl with a cracking pair of knockers, which she very kindly let me feel on one drunken night out after work. Despite her obvious assets however, Kirsten was not the most authoritative expert on football, and would turn up to work slightly worse for wear on a fairly regular basis. Having said that, audience figures held up well with Kirsten at the helm and Kelvin made it perfectly clear he didn't mind if she fluffed her lines, but all hell would break loose if she wasn't showing enough cleavage. And Kelvin on the rampage was an awesome sight.

Once, when I was moved onto the news desk, I saw him stomping down the office bellowing at the top of his lungs.

'Where's that fucking news desk! Bunch of cunts! Those fuckers are for the fucking high jump!'

I loved seeing Kelvin in full swing – he would steam around the office as if he had a rocket up his arse. As the man behind some of the most memorable tabloid headlines in history, he had a well-earned reputation of being able to deliver a tongue-lashing that could slice through suits and make grown men tremble. I literally had to stop myself from bursting into applause as he marched up to the news desk. Instead, I smiled. He glared at me.

'What the fuck are you smiling at you fucking nonce? Who the fuck are you anyway?! Where's the fucking news editor, you worthless piece of shit!'

Before I had time to answer, the news editor who had somehow screwed up the last broadcast appeared, was shouted at by Kelvin until he was reduced to tears and left the office never to return.

I was always surprised that people feared him. I was aware of his fearsome reputation but it wasn't as if he was ever going to hit you. A verbal blasting is just that — nothing more. Besides, I like a man that knows his mind. And Kelvin certainly knew his mind. With him, there was no middle ground; things were right or wrong, black or white and nothing in between. Even if he was new to television and sometimes got it wrong, at least he had the courage of his convictions. On the whole, and despite the fact that sometimes I thought he could be a bit of a cock, I found him inspiring and felt driven and focused while working for him. He was also very funny with a razor-sharp wit. When the then Prime Minister, John Major came to visit the offices, both he and Kelvin stopped just opposite from the desk where I was sitting. The hugely unpopular leader of the Conservative Party looked out of the window, captivated by the sprawling view of London from the 24th floor.

'Amazing, isn't it?' he gawped, turning to Kelvin.

'Yes, Prime Minister', Kelvin replied. 'And on a clear day you can sometimes spot a Tory voter.' He was priceless.

However, mine and Kelvin's first encounter at work

was not a very happy one. I had only been working there for a couple of months when our paths crossed. He stopped, looked me up and down and then began hurling abuse at what I was wearing – well worn jeans, trainers and T-shirt, all of them from second-hand thrift stores.

'You – what's your name?' he demanded.

'Ashley Hames.'

'Well I've got news for you. Your name is no longer whatever you say it is. Your name is Mr I'm Gonna Get Fucking Fired Cos I Look Like A Shambling Shit-tip. You're not going to work in a slum,' he shouted. 'You're at a television station. Now fucking sort it out!'

Not too long after that encounter, I was coming to the end of my contract working as a documentary researcher when the Head of Programming, Bill Ridley, came up to me from around the corner.

'It's you! *It's fucking you!*'

Bill, who I liked a lot, was cryptic at the best of times, but on this occasion I was flummoxed. What had I done? Had I messed up? Was this anything to do with Kelvin?

'Get your arse in gear and into my office now!' he demanded.

Oh Christ! It didn't sound good at all. As I scuttled into his office I found Nick Ferrari standing, waiting... and then as soon as he clapped eyes on me, started shouting.

'Yes Bill, *perfect*! Yeeeessss! He's the one!'

At this point, Bill started banging his head against the wall and laughing aloud in a state of delirium. Were they drunk? What the hell was this all about? Ferrari then instructed me to stand in the middle of the room and close my eyes. Then... darkness as something was placed on my head. Seconds later everything was clear.

chapter 2
news bunny

News Bunny was a large brown and white rabbit which was brought in to raise the profile of the channel, increase its notoriety and, hopefully, its viewing figures. It soon become synonymous with Kelvin MacKenzie's L!VE TV, and as fate had conspired, I was to be the man inside the rabbit suit. By the time Ferrari and Ridley had finished with me, they had decked me out in the full furry outfit, complete with white mittens, a huge head with enormous floppy ears and large oval eyes, out of which I could see my middle-aged masters giggling furiously to themselves. The top brass – MacKenzie, Ferrari and Ridley – were all seasoned tabloid veterans, who could scarcely hide their joy at getting their hands on the scruffiest kid in the building – an over-qualified, slightly posh, Guardian-reading university graduate – and dressing him up as a cartoon character.

As the station mascot, News Bunny was charged with representing the channel at media events and to pose with Kelvin for promotional photo shoots, but chiefly to provide animated reaction behind the newsreader during live news bulletins. His brief was to react positively to good news – a thumbs-up and a merry jig for England winning a football match, a teary wiping of the eyes for a rise in the price of beer at budget time. After a while, this graduated into near chaos – England sporting triumphs turned into flag-waving, football juggling, ear-flapping celebrations, while bad news stories would end with News Bunny slumped all over the news desk in mock despair. Beneath the outfit I would be giggling away at the ridiculous situation I had now found myself in. How fucking bizarre was this?!

Unsurprisingly though, some of the news readers and news producers were not happy that their department had been transformed overnight into something of a circus. Several of them resigned, citing the fact that their journalistic integrity was now being compromised by having a six-foot-tall rabbit cavorting around in the background of the news bulletins. I guess they had a point. Others carried on through gritted teeth. This made my position slightly awkward, but despite the fact that some people felt my new position was humiliating for me, I was just grateful to have a job and thought it was harmless fun. I hadn't imagined my media career would ever involve getting kitted out as a rabbit, but sod it – if that's how it panned out, it was fine by me. There were plenty of people out there who were a lot worse off, I'm sure.

Being News Bunny also meant I would go on plenty of jaunts to take part in outside broadcasts. Any news-worthy event such as a film premiere or press conference meant I would be called to hop into action. I remember getting dressed up and greeting Mike Atherton and his losing England cricket team on their return to Heathrow

23

airport, demonstrating forward defence strokes and cover drives. I don't think they were entirely amused. Labour leader and soon-to-be Prime Minister Tony Blair was given a News Bunny handshake at the launch of his successful election campaign of 1997.

'Is this Kelvin's idea?' he enquired, laughing awkwardly as we posed in front of the cameras. I kept my mouth shut and gave it the thumbs up.

Aside from being used as a sidekick to our own reporters, I was briefed to try to muscle in on any other film crews to try and pollute their footage. News Bunny was synonymous with L!VE TV branding, so in order to boost the channel's profile, I would try to weasel my way into other broadcasters' reports by appearing in the background. After several months of this, and reporters constantly telling me to fuck off, it did become slightly wearing. I went to see Bill 'The Riddler' Ridley to see if I could perhaps be rewarded for my efforts with a more hands-on role in the newsroom. He agreed, and in between the usual furry gestures, I started writing and producing news packages. This was interrupted one day, when Bill called me over for a chat.

His plan was to put News Bunny forward as a candidate for a forthcoming parliamentary by-election. One slight problem, Bill explained, was that they wanted News Bunny to register his candidacy as 'News Bunny' rather than my real name. Would I be willing to change my name by deed poll? My reaction was to burst out laughing. I thought this would be hilarious and as far as getting my name changed to News Bunny, well... why not? Rumours went around the office that I was being paid as much as forty thousand pounds to agree to the name change. I wish! The truth was, I did it for nothing and did it gladly.

So, having legally changed my name to News Bunny,

the news team and I headed up to Staffordshire for the election. As the leader of The Official Bunny Party, it was my aim to become the first rabbit to make it into parliament. I would be campaigning under a manifesto for reducing carrot mountains and introducing new transport schemes to cut the number of road kills: sensible policies for a rabbit.

Essentially, Kelvin was using the publicity surrounding News Bunny's candidature to boost the profile of his somewhat ailing station. On arrival in Tamworth, however, things were very quiet. To liven things up, I suggested getting myself arrested as a sure-fire way of drumming up the publicity that Kelvin craved. The news editor, Dave Nicholson, who I rated as just short of useless, wasn't convinced, but after weighing up some alternative stunts, including raiding a local pet shop to liberate some fellow mammals, we opted for breaking the law.

Armed with a hastily cobbled together placard proclaiming, 'CARS ARE KILLING US, SAVE THE BUNNY!' I planted myself in the middle of the road and proceeded to stop traffic from passing through town. Cars began piling up and beeping their horns. A crowd of drunken lads spilled out of the nearby pub and began chanting their support. It was starting to get a bit rowdy to say the least. Photos were snapped for the local newspaper, and our camera crew captured the scenes as the police arrived. I was pulled to one side by the cops and warned that if I went back out onto the street then I would be arrested. They were true to their word, and, on returning to the road, I was brusquely shoved into the back of a police car and driven down to the local police station, still dressed in my furry outfit.

On arrival, I took off my rabbit head to be charged and fill in various forms.

'What's your name, son?'

'News Bunny,' I replied.

'Don't take the piss my boy; the joke's over now.'

Luckily I was able to show the duty officer my credit card which had now been registered with my new identity. He looked at it, then back to me, then took a deep breath.

'News Bunny it is then. Sign here.'

Before long, a buzz was going round the police station with word of News Bunny's arrival. Various coppers started quizzing me on my campaign manifesto and suggested that getting arrested hadn't been such a good idea for a prospective parliamentary candidate.

'Do you have a criminal record?'

'No.'

'You will have now, son. Follow me.'

In next to no time I was ushered into a holding cell, carrying my furry head but otherwise still dressed up as a rabbit. After a couple of hours spent reading wall graffiti, the door opened and a policeman walked in with a plate of – you'd better believe it – carrot cake! It seemed I could count on the local coppers for their vote, but the only trouble was that the vote count was taking place later that evening. As I munched down my gratefully received nosh I was starting to worry that candidate Bunny would still be behind bars when his moment of election glory arrived. Kelvin would be fuming. This was our big moment and I had gone and ruined everything.

Behind the scenes though, company lawyers were battling to secure my release. And back in the offices at L!VE TV, Kelvin had stopped off at the transmission gallery to watch a live feed of the footage of my arrest. I was later told that he proclaimed it as, 'the best fucking piece of television I've ever seen in my life!'

Phew – all was not lost then. Ordering all hands on

deck to get News Bunny released, Kelvin was obviously determined to see his pet mascot freed for election night. Sure enough, an hour later the door to my cell opened once more and I was free to depart. I had been charged with obstructing a public highway and released on bail, due to appear at the local magistrate's court in a month's time.

I would worry about that later. For now, I had to make my way to the town hall and take to the stage with the other parliamentary candidates to hear the election results. When I got there, the place was awash with journalists and local campaigners. I teamed up with my film crew and was then interviewed about my prison experience by our reporter, Wendy Turner, better known as the sister of television presenter Anthea Turner (and I assumed hired purely on the basis that she looked a bit like her). As News Bunny did not speak, I simply responded with a series of ear strokes, shrugs and thumbs up, while Wendy 'translated' for the cameras. It was utterly surreal. I then marched up behind the BBC stage where presenter Jeremy Paxman was interviewing the candidates from the three main parliamentary parties. As I clambered around in the background in a clumsy attempt to get News Bunny onto the BBC broadcast, Paxman spotted me and mentioned that, 'News Bunny, who was until recently residing at Her Majesty's Pleasure, is now in attendance.'

Job done. Next, all the candidates were summoned on stage to hear the results. Out of thirteen candidates, News Bunny finished a very respectable ninth, racking up an impressive 89 votes. As I congratulated the winning candidate, Labour's Brian Jenkins, I could only think of how very different life could have been if I hadn't got arrested. Those wasted five hours spent in a police cell could have been time spent pressing the flesh and getting me the extra 27,000 votes that could have taken News Bunny to victory. It had been a close run thing, but for the time being, this 24-carrot guy would have to return to his usual day job.

And so, the following day, I arrived back at L!VE TV. As I opened the doors to the office and began the long walk down the corridor towards the studios, I saw Kelvin MacKenzie coming the other way. I'd heard about his 'best fucking piece of television' comment and was looking forward to a pat on the back from the top dog.

'Morning Kelvin.'

'Morning.'

And that was that! Both of us walked on. Surely he could have at least passed on a 'well done mate'... something. *Anything!* But another lesson learnt: don't get into the television industry if you need a well done or a thank you. Kelvin had an ego big enough to cast a shadow over Docklands itself, and he was in no mood to inflate mine. Fair enough, we're all different.

At least Kelvin did provide me with the Mirror Group's top lawyer to help prepare me for the forthcoming court case where I faced charges of obstructing a public highway. I was keen to arrive at court and take to the stand dressed as my new name would have suggested, but my lawyer quickly advised me that if I did, I would be held in contempt of court and would almost certainly be jailed. And so, on the day of the trial I arrived back in Staffordshire dressed in my only (non-rabbit) suit and ready to face the judge with my sensible face on.

'Would the defendant please rise and state his name and address.'

I stood up to address the court.

'News Bunny, Battersea, London.'

The judge's face darkened.

'Don't be ridiculous. You're showing contempt for court. This is serious. Please state your real name given to you at birth.'

Before I could respond, my lawyer stood up.

'Your honour, my client's legal name is News Bunny. He recently changed his name by deed poll to News Bunny and would be deceiving the court if he was to give his name as anything else.'

The judge glared at me. 'Mr Bunny, could you explain the circumstances surrounding your arrest?'

News Bunny was sentenced to a year's conditional discharge and was ordered to pay costs of £50. I had avoided jail and celebrated my success outside the court with a bottle of champagne and a television interview with *BBC West Midlands Today*. News had spread about my local origins – I was on the front page of the Shropshire Star, and back at home, my Dad found himself having to field phone calls from curious journalists. When asked about my background, he responded with the rather mundane, 'He was born in Stourport, moved to Bridgnorth at an early age and attended Shrewsbury School.' See, now I bet you're glad I didn't bore you with details of my early life.

Kelvin meanwhile, was revelling in the humiliation he had caused the original 'shambling shit-tip', giving a series of radio and television interviews telling anyone who would listen that due to my arrest I would no longer be able to change my name back. According to him, now that I had a criminal record, I was doomed forever to be known as News Bunny. Luckily, this turned out to be completely untrue. Sometime later, I bumped into Kelvin having now returned to my given name and asked him why he had insisted on telling people I was stuck as News Bunny.

'Never let the truth get in the way of a good news story,' came the reply.

After that, I never did read tabloid newspapers in quite the same way.

chapter 3
topless darts

Following my court appearance, I went back to work
feeling that, by standing for parliament, changing my
name, getting arrested and facing the very real threat of
going to jail, I had gone well beyond the call of duty. And
so, a couple of weeks later, I went to see Bill Ridley to ask
once again if I could perhaps move on from being a
cartoon character and start making some television. Bill
had always given me extra bits and pieces to do and he
understood that I was now keen to start making headway. He also rated my ability to come up with ideas and
do things a little bit differently – something he valued as
an important quality when working under tight budgets.
He suggested I take on the mantle of producing and
directing *Topless Darts* – the station's flagship show,
featuring, would you believe, bare-breasted girls playing
darts – accompanied by a voiceover with more double
entendres than a weekend with Benny Hill.

'Bill, I'd love to do it. Does that also mean I get a

raise?'

'No mate,' came the reply. 'Your raise will be in the fun quotient.'

I couldn't argue with that. Well, I could have done, but to be honest, money had never been a real part of my motivation. More fun sounded good to me, so I accepted the job and left the office having been instructed to come up with a new series of *Topless Darts*. This job was just getting better and better.

Later on that week, Bill and I settled on an idea of how to approach the new series: instead of being simply *Topless Darts*, each new show under my direction would be themed by its location, kicking off with *Topless Darts on Ice*. A few phone calls later and it was all sorted: my first series would be filmed at Queensway ice rink in West London, with the rather obvious aim of getting maximum nipple erection from contestants clad in nothing more than G-strings and high heels.

After a successful shoot, I later showed the finished product to Bill. He labelled it a triumph and suggested I start thinking about the next series. *Topless Darts at the Ballet, Topless Darts at the Circus,* and *Topless Darts: the Stone Age Years* were duly completed. My final series was tied in with England hosting the European Football Championships – *Topless Darts at The World Cup* was born, featuring a dwarf – Rusty Goffe – as the referee, and cutaway shots of thousands of cheering fans; shots which, due to only several of my mates turning up to filming, I had to steal from real football matches. Naturally, the girl representing England won all of her matches with ease. Germany, on the other hand, never got a look in.

By this time, I was also starting to produce other shows for which L!VE TV were to become infamous, including *The Weather in Norwegian* (starring Nordic blonde Anne Marie Foss, giving the weather forecast in a bikini) and *Britain's Bounciest Weather* – the weekend weather presented by a dwarf (Rusty again) bouncing on a trampoline in an increasingly desperate attempt to reach up towards Scotland. Another show under my umbrella was a spoof review of the day's financial activity called *Tiffany's Big City Tips*. This was essentially a strip tease delivered by the rather tantalising model Tiffany Banister. Tiffany had to be one of the dizziest girls I had ever met, but sadly she was also one of the most frigid. Anne Marie, the weather girl, was, on the other hand, far more accommodating... after getting herself a boob job, she allowed me a close inspection of her new chest – excellent work, indeed. As for Rusty the dwarf, a middle-aged married man with two kids... well, I'm afraid I never got to know him intimately. But hey, one out of three I could live with.

As you can probably tell by the types of shows that fell under my jurisdiction, the programming at L!VE TV was leftfield entertainment to say the least. As a company though, we were still struggling to get any meaningful share of the television audience, but I consoled myself with the knowledge that I was still learning my trade and, besides, I was having a blast.

I also liked and related to Kelvin's vision. When, one day, a trade magazine landed on my desk, I flicked through it to find a list of all the cable television companies, together with a written summary from their chief executives, explaining what they stood for and what kind of programming they aspired to make. Most had written long appraisals of company objectives, future shows and audience profile. Kelvin had written one word: 'fun'.

As Bill had promised, my own particular fun quotient

had indeed risen since I'd been given the flesh-filled chalice of *Topless Darts*. Having been there for nearly two years I felt that I had still more to offer. One day, I heard that the producer in charge of late night programming was moving on, and I decided to ask for his job. It was a long shot – most of the other heads of department were a good few years older than me with considerably more experience. By now though, I was one of the veterans of the station and a producer in my own right. The turnover of staff was very high, with many people using it as their springboard after around six months to work on terrestrial television where the budgets and the wages were far higher. So I also had loyalty on my side. I went to see Nick Ferrari and staked my claim. Ferrari wavered. I said I was prepared to take on the extra responsibility for a nominal salary rise. A hand was offered. I had the job. Done deal.

The extra work load was a small price to pay for a job title – Head of Sex – that made all my friends green with envy. Being Head of Sex, I was now in charge of producing the entire station's output from ten in the evening until two in the morning – four hours filled with a raft of sex-oriented programmes, including *Painted Ladies* (naked girls painting themselves), *Private Dancer* (a strip-tease), *Exotica Erotica* (sex films), *The Sex Show* (a magazine show about sex), and the wonderfully named *I've Got Wood* (topless girls trying their hand at carpentry). This also meant I was working virtually every day with glamour girls – something I was rapidly becoming very familiar with. Most of the girls made their living through nude modelling, stripping, by appearing in porn films or indeed, on the type of TV shows that I was now in charge of making. Now the job really was getting interesting.

I was under no illusions – this was no ordinary television. Head of Sex meant I was now the proud purveyor of soft porn. I mean, let's be honest here, I was making smut. People at home were not watching this for high production values: our audience was made up of lads, probably drunk, and quite possibly flicking one off the wrist. Our audience, not to put too fine a point on it, was a bunch of wankers.

So did that make me a pornographer? Probably. Did that concern me? Not one bit. What mattered to me was that finally I had found something at which I felt I could excel – combining sex and television.

Looking at my past, I could never have foreseen that I would have taken to the job with such natural ease – up until my arrival at L!VE TV, I'd never felt that sex was much of a driving force in my life. In fact, my sexual development up until my early twenties was entirely unexceptional: a few pre-teen snogs, losing my virginity at seventeen, getting a bit more confident in the bedroom during university, a couple of long-term love affairs, and several frustrating bouts of no action whatsoever.

My first time was when I took off with my then girl-friend for a weekend break in Oxford. In the evening, we got back to our B&B after a few drinks and went to bed for the strict purpose of 'doing it'. Within minutes I was dealing with a condom catastrophe. Why had I not practised putting on a fucking Johnny before? God, I can be stupid... it's a struggle at the best of times. For a slightly immature, semi-drunk virgin it was like a severe dyslexic trying to do The Times crossword. In what felt like hours later, having accomplished the seemingly impossible; I then attempted to insert a now less than fully erect penis into the vagina of my first true love. Jesus! Where the hell is it? As I lay on top of her, I dug deep and attempted to cover up my utter humiliation with some ill-judged humour.

'Ok Ruth, is it left or right?' (Left)

'Up or down?' (Down a bit)

'It's still not working.' (Down a bit more)

'Is that it? (Sort of)

And then, finally I am inside. But as I started moving in and out of my girlfriend, I was filled with a real sense of anti-climax. It just didn't really feel that great. I mean, it was OK, but it didn't exactly rock my world. It was just... vaguely pleasant. As I rocked back and forth I was starting to wonder what the big deal was all about. I think the only reason I carried on was to get it over and done with. Ruth meanwhile, lay back looking sweet but I think felt a little sorry for me.

In, out. In, out.

Oh my god, I don't believe this – I'm actually starting to feel a bit bored!

In, out... in.

Fuck it, I'm gonna fake my orgasm and get it over with.

So I did. And that's how it ended, with me then sloping off to the toilet to dispose of the rubber thinking how much more exciting wanking was than the real thing. I mean, at least then you could get stuck in, concentrate and cum.

Back in bed, I remember blurting out a few apologies and keeping up some sense of bravado with encouraging words to the effect that, with a little practise, things would doubtless get a bit better in the bedroom. But I never did get the chance to make perfect. Ruth dumped me within a few weeks. I later heard that at the time I lost my virginity, when I was led to believe that she too was a virgin, she had in fact been sleeping around and had already racked up a wealth of experience with other men. Hmm, that was fucking annoying. But I guess it taught me a lesson: it always seems to be men who get the bad rap for being unfaithful, but sometimes as I had just found out, girls can be a little bit naughty too. I wouldn't say this experience destroyed my faith in women, but it certainly made me view them with a bit more cynicism. I imagine that contributed to the fact that I was not to have another meaningful relationship until about four years later.

In my mid twenties, I began a flurry of one night stands. From then on, apart from the very rare interruption of having a girlfriend, my sex life began to consist of weekend bed-hopping, usually when extremely drunk. I was, and I suppose still am, your classic binge drinker. For me, booze was a very necessary addition to the social mix, to help get over an innate shyness. I'm not one of these alpha-male types that get dressed up, cruise up to girls and spin out some cheesy chat-up line. That just seemed a bit arrogant to me. I needed a hefty dose of the old fighting juice to give me the confidence to stop caring about the fact that I might suffer rejection – any cold shoulder meant I could simply stagger on elsewhere and try someone else.

On the whole though, I found that most girls, if they were single and you made some vague sense, were all too willing to go to bed with you. This meant I ended up sleeping with a fair amount of girls. If we're talking numbers, well, put it this way, at the time – which was about ten years ago now – I remember sitting in a pub with a friend of mine and he asked me how many girls I'd slept with. I couldn't remember. That's depressing, I thought. I knew it was well over fifty, probably less than a hundred, but couldn't recall the exact number.

The fact that I'd lost count was a bit soul-destroying. It meant that the girls, even the few that I had fallen in love with, had lost their place on my internal radar. They'd all just merged into a series of meaningless experiences. I felt like I had crossed an invisible line where you have sex with say, five to ten girls, then fall in love, get married, have kids and live a happy, settled life. It was a sinking feeling that, in some way, the boat had left without me and I was no longer a decent catch: I now had baggage. Even worse, I guess that now you can add a nought onto those figures. *I wish.* No, I can't honestly put a figure on it, but it's somewhere in the hundreds – and that's a *lot* of awkward morning-after conversations.

I'm also quite surprised I ever ended up with such an appetite for sex, bearing in mind how excruciating my first time had been. Despite that poor start, I wasn't put off and was keen to learn. And like most other things, the more you do it, the better you get. I guess the first time you dip your wick, unless you're a born Don Juan, you're never exactly going to move mountains. But nowadays things have changed and yes, I do love sex. Wanking still comes a close second though.

chapter 4
sex and drugs and rock and roll

Back at L!VE TV, things were starting to go tits up, so to speak. I was still as proud as punch with my best-job-title-in-the-world, but the station itself was being threatened with closure. It was towards the end of 1999 and many of the top brass, including the top triumvirate of Kelvin MacKenzie, Nick Ferrari and Bill Ridley had now left. Viewing figures were hovering at a critical low and crisis management meetings meant that members of staff feared for their futures.

I wasn't too worried about losing my job – I had been at L!VE TV for nearly three years and was comfortable there – possibly a bit too comfortable. Perhaps redundancy would open up some new opportunities and give me the kick up the arse I probably needed. And one cold November day, the kick up the arse came. I arrived at the office and everyone was summoned to a staff meeting: our contracts would be terminated that day. With no further ado, we were all instructed to get our belongings, say our goodbyes and leave the building. Not exactly the best way to start your day. People reacted differently to the news – some were delighted that being made redundant meant they would get a cash windfall, and others were genuinely upset because they would now be out of work. I felt ready to move on – maybe now it was time to get a proper job. I mean, let's face it; I wasn't really cut out for a career making soft porn, was I? I still had my doubts.

For the next few months I grew increasingly worried about where the next pay cheque would come from. It was fine to sit back, reassess and take a bit of time out, but I still needed to live. Then, one day at home, I spied a newspaper advert for the job of producer for a music show at the BBC. Music had always been a big part of my life so I was hopeful that this could give me a new direction. My CV was sent and I was selected for interview. And this time I even prepared for it. I requested a copy of the show so I would know a bit about what kind of programme it was. The show was called *Inside Tracks* and was broadcast on what is now BBC Three, presented by Sean Hughes, the Irish stand-up comic and writer, who was well-known at the time as a team captain on BBC2's comedy music show, *Never Mind the Buzzcocks*.

To be honest, *Inside Tracks* was a pretty depressing sight. The format of the show was a combination of chat with guest musicians and off-beat live music performances. It seemed to me that there were obvious problems: Sean seemed fairly morose, the set was dark and dingy and the music was very leftfield and would have only appealed to an elite few. Me? I was bored after just five minutes.

The job interview was with Mark Cooper, one of the BBC music big wigs and executive producer of the highly successful *Later...With Jools Holland*. I walked in and after the usual small talk he asked me what I thought of the tape I'd been sent. I hesitated for a second – then I just thought, Fuck it, I'm gonna tell the truth here.

'I thought it was pretty shit really. I was bored after a few minutes. Sean seems fucked off rather than enjoying himself. The music was pretty rank. I wouldn't watch it.'

It turned out that honesty was the best policy – Mark didn't like the show either and wanted to employ someone to make some fairly radical changes. After a fairly brief discussion the interview was over and, just a few days later, I got a phone call offering me the job. My worries were over – I'd be back working in TV.

Working with Sean took my life away from titillating television and into the world of music. While Mark and I thought the show needed a re-vamp, Sean believed *Inside Tracks* was fine how it was and didn't want me rocking the boat. Sean, you see, had a very particular taste in music – which ranged from the obscure to the deeply unpopular. I was basically an indie kid with a love of twisted pop – but nothing too far from the mainstream. At the time I was listening to bands like Suede, Pulp, the Smiths, Stone Roses, Nirvana, Oasis – bands that most people my age would be fairly familiar with.

Sean though, had a deep-seated suspicion of anything that was remotely successful – the exceptions to this rule were the more critically acclaimed, older figures like Julian Cope and Nick Cave, but anything that breached the charts was likely to be dismissed as trite rubbish. Sean took his music a bit too seriously, which was probably the reason so few people were actually bothering to tune in. But to his credit, Sean reluctantly agreed to my request in giving the show a more popular spin. He was also far happier with me when I succeeded in moving the filming venue away from the depressing basement jazz club which we were using in Chelsea and into the brighter, more swish venue of The Church studios in

Crouch End. The Church was a great location – it was owned by Dave Stewart from Eurythmics and had live music facilities, a modern studio with guitars littered across the floor and walls covered in gold and silver discs. It looked fantastic. More importantly for Sean, who enjoyed a lie-in, it was a mere stone's throw away from where he lived. And it was good for me too, as I ended up shagging the studio manageress. Yep, life was starting to get good again.

As the show's producer, I was very aware that a happy Sean made for a far better show. Although he could be a grumpy bastard, enjoyed a moan and liked complaining a lot, we got on really well and I thought he was a lovely bloke. We would hang out together after the shows and soon we became solid drinking partners. Sean, like me, enjoyed a drink.

Along with good moods all round, we also started to attract some good guests.

One of my favourite shows featured Babybird, Elastica and Terry Hall from The Specials. We concentrated on featuring what we considered credible bands, but made an effort to help give exposure to young and up and coming bands like The Wannadies and Coldplay. In fact, I'm told we gave Coldplay one of their first ever breaks on television and now they're one of the biggest bands in the world (sorry about that, world). Back then they were just starting out and we were airing a clip of their new video for *Yellow*, the song that would become their first hit. I remember them being a ridiculously polite bunch of quite posh young men. They were also very indecisive. When I asked them what song they wanted to play live to close out the show, it sparked off an intense band discussion which lasted an age. I was expecting a one word answer but somehow got caught up in a very anal debate with Chris Martin over the merits of each particular song, acoustic versus electric guitar, sonic arrangements. Yawn. Eventually I had to put a stop to it and said we needed to get on with the programme and could they just pick one. *Today please*. I can't even remember which one they picked – and I cared even less of a toss at the time. Imagine how long it must have taken Chris and Gwyneth to come up with a name for their first-born child. *And they finally plumped for Apple?*

Meeting famous people was something I was never particularly fazed by. Just like I had found myself at ease with soft porn actresses, I never really found much to get excited about by so-called celebrities. I remember filming at the Soccer Six charity event at Chelsea Football Club and being surrounded by hordes of TV personalities and being slightly disappointed at how normal they all seemed. Cat Deeley I remember nothing about apart from the fact that I thought she had a very hairy face. Gail Porter was very small but cute. Robbie Williams seemed exactly how he does on the telly – cocky and likeable, but too busy to give us an interview. Presenter Jamie Theakston was very tall with a strangely small head. Ant and Dec who I'd interviewed a couple of years before were true gents. Rod Stewart looked a bit silly in shorts. Model and now actress Kelly Brook was the only one that stood out a mile, with genuine film star looks. It came as no surprise to me that she later left London to try her luck in Hollywood. The girl is a right old stunner – I only wish I'd got her number.

What always surprised me about the guests who appeared on the show was how lame they were when we invited them out for a drink after the recording. I was an old school reader of the NME and Melody Maker and loved hearing tales of rock 'n' roll debauchery, so I was expecting our rock star and celebrity guests to give me a dose of that dream... but it never happened. It was such a letdown. As a teenager I had also fantasised about being on *Top of the Pops*: I'd always wanted to be in a band but due to a complete absence of any musical ability, that ambition had faded. But now that I was at last a part of the music biz, I was keen to rekindle those aspirations. I had read Motley Crüe's 'The Dirt' and held it up as some kind of lifestyle bible. But after the shows, with the notable exception of Elastica's Paul Jones, everyone would tend to go home after a few beers, leaving just me and Sean to fight the good fight.

During this time I was earning good money and spending every penny of it. I was going out a lot, drinking with friends, hanging out at my local boozer, attending gigs and checking out new bands. I was doing my best to live the rock 'n' roll dream in my own way... and starting to get a taste for cocaine. Coke had always played a big part in the media and music industry, and I now had a foot in both camps. It never became a daily occurrence but weekends were seldom without the accompaniment of a wrap of toot. This was nothing particularly exceptional – at the time, London was ablaze with the stuff and still is. Most of the people I knew were doing it on a fairly regular basis, and I was no different. Cocaine was all about excess; not just because it meant you could fit in more action, more venues, more music, more beers, more of everything, but because it gave me the confidence to talk to girls. It makes you feel like you can talk to anyone at anytime about anything. The truth is that I was almost certainly spouting a load of nonsense, but at the time it all made perfect sense. This meant that I had far fewer problems in chatting up women, and my strike rate went up accordingly.

As I was approaching the age of thirty however, the hangovers were starting to become troublesome. I also quickly became annoyed by the fact that if ever I had a weekend out on the town without any gear it would leave me feeling restless and bored. Before, drinking had always been enough to inspire my debauchery and silliness. Now it wasn't. That frustrated me and I was beginning to miss the innocence of a drug-free night out.

Work was going well though, and my boss – Mark – let me know that he thought my changes to the show had pulled it out of the doldrums. Unfortunately, it wasn't to last. One day I was called into Mark's office and was told that the BBC was no longer going to commission *Inside Tracks*. The next show would be our last. That's how quickly you can be out of a job in TV world. I was gutted, especially as it was vastly improved and was now starting to become a decent and relevant show. But the decision to decommission the show, it turned out, had been made months ago: I was on my way out of the Beeb.

That night I went to the BBC bar in Great Portland Street to have a quick consolation drink and got talking to the bloke standing next to me. He asked me where I worked, so I told him about *Inside Tracks* and lamented the fact that it was now being tossed onto the scrap-heap and leaving me out of a job. I was asked what my future plans were.

'I'm going to hunt down the producer of Top of the Pops, knock him out and then take his job,' came my brazen reply.

Turns out I was speaking to none other than Chris Cowie, then producer of *Top of the Pops*. He laughed and invited me to email him my CV which I later did. Luckily, as things turned out, he never replied.

chapter 5
playboy bunnies and
texan buddies

'Are you doing anything at the moment, Ashley?'

'No'.

And so began the conversation that would end up with me travelling to Texas, hanging out with a homeless alcoholic and former drug dealer, meeting and making love to a Playboy Bunny, and freaking out on drugs in the middle of the road thinking I had just died and gone to heaven.

The man on the end of the phone was Darren Bender. I had known him for a few years now, and despite his unfortunate surname, he was someone I had a great deal of time for. Darren was the commissioning editor of late night Channel 4, then known as 4Later. I had worked with him briefly before, filming a short documentary about the use and abuse of cocaine – a not entirely successful film, mainly due to the fact that I had ended up getting extremely high while behind the camera.

Now, he explained, he was looking for someone to go filming in Texas. Since leaving the BBC, I had been kicking my heels for a couple of months and loved the idea of going to the States for the first time. He wanted a wild journey filmed in the form of a video diary to make a one hour film called *Bad Trip*. He was also keen to make use of new digital technology which had led to the introduction of simple but broadcast quality cameras. Basically, this meant you could do away with a cumbersome camera crew. Digital cameras were great for making documentaries on the cheap and they were ideal for capturing spontaneous intimate moments. I liked the idea of being a completely independent documentary maker, travelling alone with no-one to look after but myself. He then asked if I could leave at short notice. No problem.

Darren was confident I could deliver a good film, but was concerned about what sort of narrative I could spin in order to make it coherent. What, he asked, could be my motivation for going to Texas? At that moment, a friend of mine walked past the door.

'Hey John,' I called out, 'why would I be want to go to Texas?'

'Err. No idea mate.'

'Come on,' I implored, 'just make something up.'

'OK. It's because you're obsessed with The Texas Chainsaw Massacre and you want to find out if Texas is a mental place inhabited by freaks and weirdoes.'

That'll do nicely. Cheers.

A week later, I landed in Austin, Texas, alone and armed with a small digital video camera. I'd done a few stints in front of camera at L!VE TV for various news reports (even without the bunny suit), but this was more full-on. I decided there and then to stay away from traditional 'presenting'. It always seemed to me that most TV presenters spoke in an annoyingly quick and ultra-animated way. That, coupled with the fact that they usually wore shiny expensive shirts meant I thought they ended up as people I couldn't possibly relate to. My aim was to document my experiences in as honest a way as possible. I was fully prepared to say and do exactly what I wanted even if it might make me look like a bit of a prick. My thinking was that if I was to be on camera, I might as well be myself and get criticised for that, rather than try and portray some 'fake' personality and get pilloried for something I was not. My other plan was very simple – seek out adventure and film it. Oh, and to sticking to the brief, occasionally mention *The Texas Chainsaw Massacre*.

On my first day I decided to toughen myself up for the job in hand by going to get a tattoo. Outside the tattoo shop I looked around for someone to handle the filming and this lad shouted out towards me – he was about my age, around thirty, with blonde hair and piercing blue eyes. He had no front teeth, was visibly drunk, and appeared to be homeless. I thrust the camera into his hands and asked him to point it towards me while I delivered a piece to camera explaining that I had just arrived in Austin and was now off to get marked for life.

Afterwards, sporting my new tattoo, I hooked up again with my new friend whose name I learnt was Chris. He had been homeless for several years. His story was shocking: he had once been a drug dealer selling speed and become addicted to the drug himself. During his downward spiral, he lost all his money, lost his apartment and got thrown out onto the streets. He was gay and he'd had family problems because of his sexuality. His best friend had died of an AIDS-related illness but Chris was lucky and tested negative, although 'lucky' isn't probably the best way to describe him. Mentally though, he had suffered a lot and had now become an alcoholic.

Chris was great fun to hang out with and I admired the fact that he had absolutely no sympathy for his own condition. We spent several days together, sometimes filming, sometimes not, and I grew to like him a lot. I don't know why it is, but certainly where someone like Chris is concerned, and also today in the people I like and the subjects I enjoy filming, I feel constantly drawn to outsiders; people on the margins of society. Even though my own upbringing was a happy one in a fairly sound and secure middle class environment, I naturally gravitate towards those who have perhaps been less fortunate. That also applies to the people I have always admired – in the field of music for instance, my heroes were Morrissey, Bowie, Kurt Cobain, Jarvis Cocker: figures that had achieved success through their own particular idiosyncrasies.

Chris was more of an outsider than anyone I had ever known before. He literally had nothing. For the moment though, he had me following him about with a camera and that meant a lot. After around a week of hanging out with him, I saw him in the distance talking to someone on the street. When Chris saw me he started shouting, 'There he is. That's the guy! Ashley! Ashley!'

He was pointing me out to a stunning twenty-something girl called Jeannie, who it turns out just happened to be a former Playboy Bunny. Say no more – Jeannie was gorgeous. She was a mixed race girl of Thai and Swedish extraction, with fantastically pert boobs, a friendly face and a figure to die for... an absolute vision. She had popped out for a meal and had seen Chris feeding pigeons on the street and so thought it might be a decent thing to do to offer him something nice to eat as well. Jeannie was joined by her friend Dale, an older man with whom she shared a house. Both Jeannie and Dale were committed Christians and they saw their role in helping Chris as a very much a part of their Christian lifestyle. How being a Playboy Bunny went down with God I had no idea, but I for one liked it.

During their meal with Chris, Dale and Jeannie had discussed the possibility of taking him to rehab. They now suggested to Chris that he went back with them to their house where they would help clean him up and get him ready. I switched my camera on and started to film. Chris was already starting to appear nervous but Jeannie persuaded him that rehab would help sort out his problems and eventually he relented. The next day, we took Chris to Austin Rehabilitation Centre. I was extremely sad to see Chris leave. I had let him stay in my hotel room and had spent over a week with him. He'd always been great company, and despite his poverty, never once pestered me for money and never betrayed my trust. That makes him a pretty sound bloke in my eyes.

After leaving Chris in rehab, I was left to carry on with the rest of my documentary. The next day I ended up talking to a waitress who I liked the look of and who I shall call Amber. I invited her for a drink and we went for a night out in Austin. Amber was brilliant fun, very sexy and wild. We ended up back at the hotel and after we had sex, I immediately grabbed the camera and held it overhead.

'So how was that for you?' I asked, panting for breath.

'You fuck like a beast!' came the reply.

Hmm, I'll take that as a compliment. My years of practice were starting to pay off. If possible, filming got even more full-on the next day when I went round to Amber's house to meet some of her friends. I noticed a large fruit bowl on the kitchen table overflowing with weed. It turned out to be one of the strongest types of skunk available to humanity, known locally as 'Texan Bud'. Unfortunately, I didn't know that at the time, and as I swallowed down lungfuls of the stuff, Amber looked at me as though I was completely insane and advised me to go easy.

'It's not working though, I can't feel anything,' I said as I sucked down on a huge bong rammed with the evil-looking skunk.

Less than half an hour later and it well and truly hit me. I was utterly, severely off my face... incredibly, outrageously fucked out of my head. But not in a good way. Let's get this straight: I can drink for England, stagger about, be sick, piss in my pants... anything; but my mind always stays fairly intact. This though, was different. I had smoked a fair amount of weed before, the occasional bit of skunk; but nothing like as strong as this – and not anywhere near this quantity, and not through a bong. This was starting to go wrong – it was not a pleasant sensation. In fact, that's understating things by a huge degree: it was a fucking horrible feeling. Paranoia raced through me in waves and my head felt like it was going to explode. I was starting to hear bits of my brain collapse. Who were these people? What did they want with me? Why was that camera pointing at me? Where the hell was I? I fell onto a sofa and pretended to be asleep, ignored everyone and everything and waited for the moment to pass. By having my eyes closed it just felt like I was constantly freefalling and spinning straight to hell.

After what seemed like hours, but was probably a lot less, I was still fucked. The moment had evolved into what seemed like a permanent state of being. The fear of never being able to return to your normal self will be very familiar to anyone who has suffered a bad comedown off drugs. This feeling however, was way worse than just the normal comedown. I felt like my mind had tripped a switch – I was in the midst of a full blown panic attack; something I had never experienced before and that hit me like a hurricane. I was convinced I had would be incarcerated in a mental hospital with the diagnosis 'FUCKED' hanging above my bed in big black letters.

By now, the others had all gone to bed, so I heaved myself off the sofa, opened the front door and sat down on the porch to catch my breath and try to pull myself together. As if the scene couldn't get anymore surreal, there was an almighty flash of lightning. It crashed down to earth and hit the ground right in front of my feet. What the..? Was that fucking real? *Was that really fucking real?!* In my ravaged state, I was convinced I had just been visited by God. What was happening to me? My answer was that I believed I was, in fact, dead. This – what I was experiencing and seeing around me – was my eternity. Whether it was heaven or hell, I wasn't too sure, but I decided to take a look around. And so, in a blaze of confusion, I headed off down the street, staggering around in the middle of the road not caring if cars were there or not – I was dead anyway, what did it matter if I got run over?

Suddenly I heard a voice – I was being called back inside. I headed towards the sound and was met by Amber. She immediately recognised that I was deeply disturbed (something in the eyes) and urged me to take a valium. After a brief moment of paranoia (was this really valium or was she feeding me acid?) I took the pill and felt myself heading back to some kind of normality.

At least that's what I thought. We went to bed and I lay down beside her. There then followed one of the most nightmarishly surreal ten minutes of my life as Amber transformed before my eyes into every single girl I had ever slept with. Girls who I had totally forgotten began to reappear in front of me before morphing into the next one. Not a single one was missed out – from girls who I had been in love with, to casual flings that I thought had disappeared from my brain forever; even a prostitute I had spent less than half an hour with over a decade before in a seedy Soho knocking joint. Scary. Very, very scary. Then, finally... sleep.

When I woke up the next day, I was still extremely shaken. The previous night's experience had left me feeling fragile and freaked out. I'd travelled to Texas to make a television documentary and it was starting to seem like I was taking the title of *Bad Trip* a little too literally. I resolved to put the whole episode to the back of my mind and deal with it later. At that point, I wanted to get out of Austin and discover somewhere new. I decided to call Jeannie, the Playboy model. After we had dropped Chris off at the rehab centre, she'd offered to drive me anywhere I wanted in Texas and I decided to call in the favour.

Jeannie seemed happy to see me and I was likewise pretty chuffed to hook back up with her. I eagerly jumped in beside her in her racy red sports car and after a few hours' drive; we arrived in a small town called Kerville. There were no real plans. We scouted around for a while and got ourselves a small room in the first crappy motel we clapped eyes on.

As Jeannie got ready to go out for the evening, I knew I was starting to fall for her. I'm not saying it was love, but I definitely found her damn sexy and was keen to get her into bed... not least so I could finally say, 'Yes lads, I've slept with a Playboy model'. As per normal though, I didn't really think I stood a chance – this girl had starred in various blue movies and been on the cover of Playboy magazine – she was well out of my league. I resolved to do what I normally did when faced with someone I fancied – get drunk, and make my move when I didn't care whether I got a yes or a no.

We eventually headed off out to a nearby bar; me in an England football shirt, Jeannie with her breasts struggling to remain inside a somewhat skimpy boob tube. A ton of booze saw us eventually collapsing into bed together. Annoyingly however, I was so drunk that I was incapable of making any coordinated or meaningful physical movement whatsoever, let alone having sex, and so we put our heads down and slept.

Come the morning though, I was ready for action and Jeannie was only too happy to indulge me. Brilliant! Jeannie had the most amazing body I had ever seen in my life with perfect proportions and amazingly soft and luscious skin. Oh, and did I mention her *magnificent* breasts? Natural but surgically lifted – which meant that as I looked up from between Jeannie's legs while licking her pierced clit, her boobs appeared like some kind of mirage reaching for the heavens. I had, it seemed, just discovered the Eighth Wonder of the World.

Now, back to reality. Where were those bloody condoms? Clothes went flying, my suitcase emptied, but no luck. Sex would have to wait. The problem was, Jeannie was going to have to return home that day, and I had decided that for the good of my film, I would have to continue travelling elsewhere. A slightly more frantic search was mounted but to no avail. It was not to be. Fuck it. Jeannie and I said our goodbyes and I made a mental note to return back to Austin and hook back up with her before I returned home.

And that's exactly what I ended up doing. I was now into my third week in Texas and the film was in the bag. When I got back to Austin, I called Jeannie and we met up again for my last night before returning home to

England. After an evening of pool-playing, drinking and karaoke, Jeannie and I ended up back in bed together. Jeannie, as well as being a fun and energetic personality, was no slouch in the sack. I almost had to stop myself from shouting out loud, 'Hey look everyone, I'm fucking a Playboy Bunny!' I mean, come on, this was every schoolboy's dream and somehow I had ended up living it. God, I felt like such a lucky bastard.

Some hours later, I was landing back on earth at Heathrow airport with a jolt – sex with Playboy bunnies and careering around America with a camera was now a thing of the past. Back to life; back to reality.

After completing the edit for *Bad Trip*, I was once again left wondering where life would take me next. When the show was broadcast on Channel 4 I had a very brief taste of fame, with people coming up to me in pubs and bars, telling me how much they had enjoyed the show. I was really proud of the fact that most people who had seen it didn't say they just liked it or that it was OK... they absolutely *loved* it. Most of them kept asking me the same question: 'Did you shag that Playboy Bunny?'

Jeannie, it seemed, had had almost as big an impact on the viewers as she'd had on me. The Channel 4 website also had a couple of interesting responses from viewers.

If we don't see more of Ashley Hames, I am going to come round to Channel 4 with a gun. He is very cool, laid back and perfect for late night telly.'

They weren't all positive though. Another message read as follows:

'I saw Bad Trip last night. Disgraceful – Ashley Hames stands for everything that is bad in society today.'

Ouch. I still can't make my mind up whether that was

a good or bad review though.

Despite the occasional criticism, I was satisfied that I'd done a decent job and was happy that I hadn't let myself or Darren down. When he saw the finished show, he was amused at my antics – I had filmed myself freshly post-coital, taking drugs, racing around drunk with a homeless lad and appearing in bed with a Playboy Bunny. I later heard that he tried to get the production company to rename it *Bad Trip: Boy Behaving Badly*. Unfortunately though, he was too late – the film had left the edit and was to be called *Bad Trip: Southern Discomfort*, itself a fairly accurate description of the events that unfolded.

At the time of the film's broadcast, I was still far from happy with where my career was headed – I was fed up with persistent periods of unemployment and was itching to get back to filming. As 2001 kicked off, I was once again having to sign on down at the dole office where I would pour over depressing notices for endless menial and soul-destroying jobs. Even more depressing was what happened next.

Following my return to London, my lifestyle was still pretty unhealthy and one horribly drunken night had left me dealing with the hangover from hell. I switched on the television and started watching a documentary about Adolf Hitler and the Second World War. Suddenly my mind started racing. My thought processes went something like this: 'Jesus, that Hitler guy is so fucked up; the world is so fucked up; everything is fucked; we're all fucked. Oh my God, I'm fucked: I am well and truly fucked up!'

And then: Panic. *Total panic*. This wasn't the kind of panic attack which I've since read about – where your breathing becomes strained, blood rushes to your head and you reach for the paper bag. This was something else.

I was feeling the sharp end of some kind of existential angst — if people like Hitler existed, I reasoned, then surely God didn't exist; and if God didn't exist then there was no meaning to anything. Everything was crazy. Fuck! Did that mean I was going mad? Oh my God, I was going *fucking crazy*!

As soon as the thought came to me that I was on the edge of insanity I couldn't get rid of it. Right then, in my mind, I was clinically insane. I was having *exactly* the same feelings that I'd had during my dodgy skunk smoking experience back in Texas just a couple of months before. And let me tell you this; it was the most traumatic sensation I had ever experienced. This, my friends, was *the fear*.

I had crossed the line, tripped out, and was heading inexorably towards a mental institution for the rest of my life. When it happened to me back in Texas, at least then I'd had the comfort that it had been drug-induced. This time, there had been no drugs involved. Sure, I was hungover, but I'd had hundreds of hangovers and all of them had passed without major incident. Not this time. Worse was the sinking fear that perhaps, through my constant abuse of alcohol and drugs, I had irreparably damaged my brain. This just made me even more paranoid. Fair enough if you fall over and break a leg — that can be healed. But it's not as if a doctor could just give me a new one and make everything better. I was reminded of the Pulp song, *Sorted for Es and Whiz* — the line where Jarvis phones his mother at home. In my case, it would have been 'I've left a part of my brain, in a smoke-filled room in somewhere in Texas,' rather than a field in Hampshire.

I decided to go outside, take a walk and try and get back to some kind of reality. It was too late to call a doctor but I promised myself that I would go and see one as soon as I woke up in the morning. When the similar incident had taken place in Texas, I tried to make myself forget the entire incident by filing it away in a discreet part of my brain. The fact that it could happen a second time though, meant it could happen a third, a fourth or a fifth time. That prospect was too unbearable to contemplate – I needed to try and nip this in the bud.

I was surprised I actually managed to get any sleep at all that night but I did clock in a couple of hours. When I dragged myself out of bed in the morning, I noticed the sheets were soaked through: I had wet my bed for the first time in probably twenty-five years. I didn't need a medical degree to realise that this was undoubtedly a sign of mental trauma, so I pulled myself round, made an appointment and headed off to see the doctor. When I explained to her what was happening to me, she immediately pin-pointed drug and alcohol use as the trigger for my symptoms. She also revealed that she saw several people every week with similar problems – this shocked and reassured me at the same time – at least I wasn't the only one thinking they'd gone and lost the plot. I was advised to cut out drugs completely and to lay off the booze for a while and was also given some reading information about panic attacks. When she asked if I would like to have a psychological assessment from a psychotherapist, I agreed immediately and she arranged for someone to visit my house later in the week.

I left feeling a lot better, but I knew I was in a delicate state. Slowly but surely though, my confidence returned, and by the time the psychotherapist came round a few days later, I felt pretty much OK. I let him into the house and he began by asking me the usual questions about family life (normal, happy), work (love it), love-life (disappointing), lifestyle (dubious). Towards the end of the conversation I stopped him.

'All I really want to know,' I said, 'is whether God

exists. If I can figure that out then everything will be alright.'

The therapist stopped in his tracks. Then slowly he smiled and looked at me.

'I'm afraid if I had the answer to that,' he replied calmly, 'I wouldn't be here now. I'd be dead.'

Fair enough. He then told me that I appeared to be a fully functioning, completely normal human being. I'm not sure I entirely agreed with that particular diagnosis, but the truth was that I was getting back to my usual self. I was off the drugs – for the time being – and was drinking a bit less. Over the next year or two, I still suffered occasional waves of dread/fear/angst – whatever you want to call it – but I was now able to control it and bring myself back from the brink.

I knew that the horror of a panic attack wouldn't last forever and that gave me hope and relief. I had recovered once, I had recovered again, and if it happened in the future I would just have to dig deep and get through it. For the time being, that was good enough for me. Close call. I wasn't insane and didn't fancy cashing in my chips just yet.

chapter 6
the uncomfortable truth

After the trauma of the last few months I thought I was
due a break. I had written up a couple of programme
ideas and decided to go and see Charlotte Black at
Channel 4. Charlotte had always been very good at
advising me where I should send my CV and who I should
speak to about new ideas or possible jobs in television.
After she told me my ideas were crap (they were), she
asked me if I'd heard of *Sin Cities,* a series which went
out on the UK cable and satellite channel Bravo TV. I
hadn't. Charlotte explained that it was a fairly racy,
risqué sex show which took a light-hearted, laddish look
at the world of pornography, swinging, S&M culture... in
short, anything and everything to do with adult
behaviour. It had been presented by Grub Smith, a
journalist who also wrote a regular sex column in lads'
magazine, FHM. Grub was now working on something
else, but Bravo were still keen to do another series of the
show and were looking for a new presenter. Charlotte,

who had seen my exploits in *Bad Trip*, suggested I get in touch. I rustled up a copy of *Bad Trip* and sent it to Donna Clark, the executive producer of *Sin Cities*.

A few days later, I got the call to go in and see her for a chat. She asked me how I felt at the prospect of working on a sex-oriented documentary series which would be filmed abroad in Asia, America, South America and Australia. I mean, this was the kind of question that only happened in dreams. Trying desperately to keep a straight face, I told her I was quite happy to go around the world and get paid to film a sex-orientated series. It didn't work. I was grinning from ear to ear before I finished my reply. Donna laughed and introduced me to Duncan Wilson who was going to be directing the show.

Duncan grabbed his video camera and we took a cab together to go and shoot a small screen test at a sex shop in Hoxton Square called Shh! I was instantly comfortable with Duncan behind the camera and I could sense him smirking as I rifled through all the sex toys, disingenuously wondering aloud why anyone would want to bother with them. We then did an interview with the owner and I asked her about the shop and what purpose it served – she explained that Shh! was a shop catering for women, with toys that helped to spice up their sex life, and, most important of all, help them achieve that most elusive of goals: the female orgasm.

I decided to play dumb and replied like a bit of a twat.

'But why is it so important for the woman to have an orgasm? That's never been a concern of mine.'

She looked at me as though I was some kind of Neanderthal and insisted that my attitude was one that had kept women in sexual limbo for years and that men should start caring about the feelings of women in bed, rather than selfishly concentrating on their own satisfaction. We should, she insisted, ask women what they want, use different toys, and try different positions other than just the standard missionary.

'Is there any other position?' I asked, apparently dumbfounded.

She nearly terminated the interview there and then. Duncan however, loved it. In an instant we had chanced upon a different way of looking at sex – with irreverence and knowing stupidity. We returned to the office and met back up with Donna. She explained that she had set up another screen test for the following week and would be in touch.

Sure enough, a few days later I met up with Donna in South London. After coffee and cigarettes we headed into a slightly seedy looking dungeon where we were met by a dominatrix clad in black. She started taking me around the various contraptions she had on display, while Donna filmed. After a few cheeky comments from yours truly the mistress took out her whip, suggested I was deserving of punishment and bent me over a wooden table. She hit me on the backside a few times and while it was all quite bizarre, I played up to the situation to see what I could get out of her for the camera.

'Please miss, can I have some more?' I ventured.

That was the moment I think I got the job. When it was later offered to me I was chuffed to bits. Presenting *Sin Cities* would involve travelling the world in a small team of three – me, Duncan and an assistant producer, Danny. Each show would be filmed over the course of a week and our first stop was to be Manila, capital of the Philippines. Had I landed on my feet, or what?

I had a couple of months before we set off, so to help prepare, I asked for some tapes of the previous shows, presented by Grub Smith. Grub was a few years older than me and seemed extremely confident in front of camera. It pains me to say, but he was also handsome, intelligent, witty and had a natural charm about him. Watching him in action made me feel a lot less confident. In fact, seeing Grub in action made me think that perhaps I wasn't even ready for this. The thought of presenting an entire series of 15 half-hour shows, each filmed over a week in a different city in a round-the-world trip, was a far cry from doing my one hour *Bad Trip* documentary on my own and in my own time. I couldn't let these thoughts consume me though. I was there because I'd done my time and was up for the job. In my own sometimes passive way, this was the dream I'd been chasing, though I wasn't sure if I knew it yet.

On the flight over to the Philippines, I resolved not to try to compete with Grub's style of presenting. Instead, I decided to throw caution to the wind, banish my self-consciousness and just go for it – I knew I wasn't completely useless; I knew how to give good show, and in Duncan I felt I had found a director that knew how to get the best out of me. It was game on: *Sin Cities* had landed.

When we arrived in Manila, we had a couple of free days before we started filming. Never having been big on sight-seeing or museums or anything like that, I quickly unpacked and headed off out with Duncan to see what the night-life was like. Duncan was the ideal drinking partner. In fact, his enthusiasm for a beer easily outstripped my own. He also held true to the idea that we should live the *Sin Cities* lifestyle rather than just pay lip service to it on camera. This meant that our first night was spent getting completely hammered, going to a girlie bar, wading through a sea of shots with some of the girls, and then taking a couple of them back to the hotel to share a few more fluids.

Duncan looked and behaved like he'd just walked out of the pages of Loaded magazine – he always wanted to go the extra mile, have just one more drink, one more dance, one more of everything, and if ever I made a move to bring the evening to a close I would be shot down with the reminder that, as I was now the presenter of *Sin Cities* it was part of my job to stay out and party. As jobs go, that wasn't too big a strain, and, on our first night out I willingly accepted the extra work responsibility; 'That'll be two more pints of lager please.' With the first day of filming starting the next day, sharing my bed with a Philippine girl had proven a bit of a distraction, and in preparation for my debut *Sin Cities* performance I hadn't slept a wink. Luckily for me though, the first shoot had fallen through and I could go back to bed. Perfect. I was starting to get the hang of this TV presenting lark.

A day later, we did actually get some work done. One early problem I had to confront was that *Sin Cities* showed full nudity and I had been asked in my interview if I would be comfortable being naked. This basically meant that I'd have to get the old frank 'n' beans out on camera. I wasn't entirely happy with this but felt that if the other contributors on the show were happy to be naked, then as the presenter, I too should play ball. I had no moral objection to it whatsoever; my misgivings were motivated purely by ego: I had a very average-sized penis and didn't consider it something I particularly wanted to show off. What's more, when flaccid, it was distinctly unimpressive. Remember the first time you had to whip it out in front of the doctor? We always say that the little chap shrivels up at the thought of having to show it to someone you're not about to put it in, so getting it out for a TV audience was never going to be easy. When you're in shot on TV and naked, no one is looking at your face — you can't kid yourself otherwise. By baring all, I was running a very real danger of being humiliated. Fuck it. Best way to cope with this would be to jump straight in and get it over and done with in the first week. So I did.

In Manila, the *Sin Cities* team found an erotic bakery which would make a mould of body parts and then bake it into a cake. Rather than just reporting on the existence of such an establishment, I was expected to go gonzo and get my own cake made, with my penis providing the mould. As the camera rolled and necks were craned, I could physically feel my cock virtually disintegrate as I undid my zipper.

As I looked down it was a heart-breaking sight. They could have used a thimble to take the mould and had room to spare! Despite my huge embarrassment regarding my then-miniscule appendage, the cake, albeit one mounted by what appeared to be the genitalia of a small child, was successfully made – I had negotiated the first major obstacle to my new presenting job. Getting my willy out was the only time I ever really felt self-conscious during the filming of *Sin Cities*. This was something I was never entirely able to shake off. Fortunately for me, there were times when I wasn't entirely alone in my humiliation.

When we visited Hawaii, the *Sin Cities* team was invited along to a wedding that was due to take place on a nudist beach later that day. It was, as I'm sure you'll now realise, going to be a naked wedding. When we arrived, Duncan (directing) and Danny (producing) were smiling at me in smug and sadistic anticipation, knowing I would be dreading the moment when my shorts would have to drop. But as we spoke to the happy couple, they explained in no uncertain terms that everyone, without exception, who was present at the wedding, would have to be entirely naked. Yes, *including* the camera crew. Oh, how the tables had turned! I don't think I have seen anyone look quite as petrified as Duncan and Danny did at that precise moment. With good reason – as it turned out, both of my tormentors boasted rather camera-shy little members. And with temperatures in the high 80s, there were no excuses. Sorry lads, but rules are rules.

It's difficult to explain why I was always so hung up about being naked and getting my cock out. It's just one of those things you can either do and not care less, or do because you have no choice and never be able to get over, no matter how much you want to. See, when I'm in bed with someone, I'm comfortable with my kit off, and am pretty happy with the way my body looks. There's no problem. But like most other men, I'm prone to size insecurities and dream of having that all-too-elusive extra inch. On the whole though, I would have to say I am fairly content. It could be better, but it could be a lot, lot worse. I have done plenty of research on penis size and it turns out that I am a classic case of average, standing at just less than eight and a half inches erect.

God I wish that last sentence was true. I genuinely believe that if I'd been blessed with a big cock then my sex life would have been very different and I would definitely have had far more confidence. There are times when you go to bed with someone when you feel certain trepidation about delivering a decent performance in the sack. Imagine starting up a new relationship with a very sexually confident girl; you really like her but you just can't seem to rock her world in the bedroom. You then find out her last boyfriend was Jimmy Three-Legs and it all starts to make perfect sense. I've even been in bed with a girl who, on clapping her eyes on my todger, looked up at me. 'Your willy's not very big is it?' she said. How can you possibly answer that? I hasten to add that I wasn't fully erect at that point. And trust me: by the final word of her sentence, I was almost fully flaccid. Make no mistake – it was a depressing thing to hear, and a bit rich coming from a girl with a vagina like a wizard's sleeve.

Although most girls will insist, and have always insisted to me, that size doesn't matter ('unless it's really small', is what I've been told), my own take on this is that unless a girl is being vindictive, she's far more likely to tell you what you want to hear. If you turn things on their head for a second and substitute penis size for vaginal size, well, I'm sorry, but size does matter. How many men would say they would rather encounter a large vagina than a small one? I mean, let's face it, for a man, a tight fit is far more satisfying than a loose fit, and I doubt if it's any different for a woman. Why then, while thousands of men have openly agonised over their penis size, have women yet to articulate any concerns they may have about vagina size? There is no doubt that some girls are bigger than others, and yet it's not a subject I've ever really heard anything about. I think women do worry about their vaginas, but it's been a relatively taboo subject. I suppose people are starting to talk about it finally though – 'designer vaginas' is a phrase that is now becoming a part of everyday discourse in Hollywood. Also, I think the increasing trend for girls to have babies by Caesarean section is partly to do with women wanting to keep their vaginas in trim condition for their mate. And not wanting to sound too much of a twat, I have to say that I don't see anything wrong with this at all – if you have sex with someone who has popped a few kids out of the front door, there is, shall we say, far more give.

It may sound superficial but I myself make no apologies for my own particular sexual desires and tastes – even in terms of breast size. Anything below a C cup is a bit too small for me. It's not like I'd turn my nose up at a woman with B cup boobs, I'm just saying I *prefer* larger ones. Now, if I'm saying that, and saying it honestly, then surely there are thousands of women for whom a five inch penis is somewhat disappointing. Sure, they'll make do...

but who wants to just make do?

Despite these uncomfortable truths, I've nevertheless come to the conclusion that most men are pretty similar down below – I just wish that God had made the average penis size seven and a half inches rather than the less impressive six, thereby keeping both sexes happy. I suppose, on the whole, it does ring true that if you learn how to use it, the actual size of your penis becomes less and less relevant the more proficient you become in the bedroom.

That said, cock size does to a certain degree, have a bearing on sexual performance. In terms of positions, I'm still a bit reluctant to engage in cowgirl or reverse cowgirl, simply because I'm more likely to slip out – an annoyance which can ruin the moment if you're in full flow. Don't get me wrong, those positions aren't out of my league, but if I'm going hell for leather I'm not as self-assured as I want to be. If I stick to missionary, doggy, most other positions, then it's game on. But even then, cock-size – or lack thereof – bugs me. I don't, for instance, always want to make love while having sex. Like any other red-blooded male, I sometimes like to fuck, to give a girl a good old-fashioned nailing. Frustratingly however, I think I probably fall short of being able to deliver a genuine pummelling.

I'm sure some people reading this may think I'm some kind of weirdo obsessed with cock size, rough sex, and my own sexual pleasure. And I am. But I do think that wanting to mix it up a bit is a sign of a healthy sex life. I also usually end up with girls who I find have very similar tastes to my own, many of whom like nothing more than to get fucked to within an inch of their lives, and I do my best to oblige.

I'm sure penis size will always be a real concern for men – it certainly will be for me. Then again I probably have an extremely distorted sense of my own inadequacies in this area... and also because most of the penises I have seen belong to male porn stars. They say the camera adds a few extra pounds, but trust me, most of these guys are hung like ponies.

There were a few other times when I had to bare all on camera. Naked skydiving, which we were to film a couple of weeks later in New Zealand, was a pretty disturbing experience, not least because, having never skydived before, I had to have a naked male instructor strapped to my back. Try to imagine it. I suspect Duncan could have arranged a female instructor but deliberately chose not to, the bastard. At least on this occasion, I had a decent excuse for the poverty of my penile dimensions – let me assure you, the air at 20,000 feet is very, very cold.

Back to Manila... and having munched my way through my penis cake (all two mouthfuls of it); we were coming to the end of filming in the Philippines. We spent a couple of days filming in the city of Angeles before we left. Angeles is a truly bizarre place – a former US army base now dominated by prostitution. The place is littered with titty bars, replete with topless dancers and working girls. In a particularly rundown area of town, you'll also find a well-known rickety old road called 'Blow Row', a seedy alley-way where oral sex is available for a little as five dollars.

This brings me to a tricky dilemma. I love the fun and frolics of being surrounded by topless girls or even prostitutes. However, in a third-world country like the Philippines, there is always the suspicion of dubious standards at play. 'Blow Row' was the epitome of such seediness, with young, unkempt girls hanging around beckoning you to join them inside. I felt really uncomfort-able with this – I'd had sex with prostitutes before and always felt a sense of guilt and shame in paying for sex, a guilt I hadn't yet started to be able to fully articulate. However, in a city beset with hookers and under siege with middle-aged male Westerners, this was surely the worst in sex exploitation. Our filming in 'Blow Row' was short lived — this was subject matter for a serious documentary, not *Sin Cities*.

On the subject of exploitation though, I was determined that if anyone was going to be exploited in *Sin Cities*, then that person would be me, not those members of the public who had volunteered to appear on camera for our benefit and on whom the show ultimately depended. I was happy to be the fall guy, the victim, and, as it turned out on our return to Manila, the bloke up on stage dressed as a transvestite singing a really bad Karaoke version of *Oh! I Do Like to be Beside the Seaside.*

chapter 7
getting pissed and
getting pissed on

Although I'd been warned by my doctor to steer clear of booze, abstinence was proving difficult. And when we flew off to Sydney, we were determined to experience everything that Aussie culture had to offer. We had no filming to do until 11am the following day, so Duncan and I headed off to sample what delights the city had to offer. And after the delights, we hit the pub mid-afternoon to sample their beers. It seemed like a good plan at the time. However, in a state of near-oblivion, we finished off our marathon session with a final pint at around quarter to eleven the next morning and headed off to the shoot, determined to appear sober and professional.

We were met at the door of an old warehouse by the editor of a magazine called Wet Set – a top-shelf glossy dedicated to the portrayal of girls urinating. Because we'd tipped up late, the girls, who had been drinking copious amounts of water and saving up their wee for the cameras, were now close to bursting point. We slurred an apology, pulled ourselves together and started filming. As I was interviewing a couple of the girls, the banks of their bladders began to burst and wee started pouring from their knickers. Piss-play was a fetish that I had never come across before and I couldn't really get my addled head around it – I was almost taken aback, but certainly confused as to why anyone would see this as sexually thrilling? The girls insisted that it was something they did even in their private lives, as well as for the magazine and our cameras. My reaction, as with many other of the more outlandish fetishes that I came across in the early days, was to think this was just plain weird.

How times change. Back in England a few years later, my sexual horizons had been broadened considerably by what I had experienced on the road. Had you asked me before I'd taken on the mantle of *Sin Cities* if pissing would ever feature on my sexual agenda, I would have told you a resounding no. But the more I saw and the more I understood about various sexual practices, the more comfortable I became at incorporating them into my own private life. That includes the type of behaviour I'd seen back in Sydney that day.

I remember once after a drunken night out arriving home in South London with my then-girlfriend and collapsing in a heap on the floor. As we romped around, tearing each other's clothes off, I suddenly got an irresistible urge to take a piss on her. So I did.

Fuck knows what was going through her mind, but she went with the flow (pardon the pun). My piss began to cascade down her breasts and she gathered it up in her hands, rubbing it over her body. What a sight! I invited her to do the same to me, and, punctuated by giggles, she knelt over me and weed on my chest. This was the first

72

time I had actually done anything like this and I have to confess, I didn't mind it one bit – the whole thing just seemed pretty funny.

Now, if I was reading this and I had never partaken in so-called 'water-sports' I would, possibly like yourself, be thinking 'That's a bit rank. Why would anyone want to piss on someone else as some kind of twisted sexual foreplay? It's also degrading to his girlfriend. That Ashley needs his head examined.'

What you need to understand though, is that this was (for once) someone I really loved. I adored this girl so much it was untrue, and yet I had just pissed all over her, and she over me. So what was that all about? In any other context it would have been the worst insult, but together and consensually, it was completely unexpected fun. As odd as it may sound, I would honestly say these water sport activities also had some twisted sense of romance about them. On the one hand, this was just drink-fuelled larking about. But on the other, it was more meaningful than that. By doing something a bit taboo, you and your partner share something unique, a bond, a secret, a sexual kink that you maybe wouldn't tell your friends about. That brings you closer together. I also think that in my case, indulging in water sports was a roundabout way of telling my girlfriend that I loved everything about her – not just her adequately-sized boobs, her face, her voice... even her body waste.

OK, so why didn't I just tell her this rather than get soaking wet with piss? Well, I did tell her this, but I also wanted to express it physically and sometimes that's how I did it. No one can really explain their kinks convincingly – you are either into something or you're not. And you never know until you try. So as part of my voyage on the good ship Sin Cities, I discovered that what can, at first glance, seem disgusting, debauched and degrading on the surface, can also be an honest and genuine expression of love. It's just a very particular means of expression. That said – I won't be eating anyone's shit in a hurry.

Peeing also featured quite heavily in the adult baby fetish which I was to film later on in the course of the show. A couple of years on and we arrived in Johannesburg at the house of someone I shall call Mistress Xania. I was invited to wear a nappy in order to help immerse myself in the adult baby experience firsthand. For a man in his early thirties this seemed like a questionable thing to do, but I happily obliged and stifled my giggles as Mistress Xania helped to safety pin my new nappy together. Once I was snugly fitted in and had a bib fastened around my neck, I did, to all intents and purposes, look like an overgrown baby. I wondered though, was being an adult baby just about dressing up and acting like one, or did mean getting right into character and making use of the nappy?

'Feel free to have a wee wee,' Mistress Xania explained, 'that's what babies do.'

Brilliant. But was this really something I wanted to do on camera – surely I should at least try and retain some shred of dignity? Nah, I couldn't think of any good reason why. Instead, I figured that if I was truly to get to grips with what motivated people's sexual behaviour, then I would have to experience it for myself. Well, that's my excuse anyway.

So I braced myself and concentrated. Soon enough there was a small dribble, which, as I relaxed, turned into a fully fledged slash. And what was there to say about it all? Well, I recall saying something fairly humdrum like 'Hmm, that feels quite good really... nice and warm.'

But that, for me, is kind of the point: what can, at a

distance, seem the most outlandish, weird and bizarre practice is sometimes, on closer inspection, almost normal. I say almost, because aside from the physical sensation of having warm wee sloshing around in your knickers, being all trussed up as a baby did leave me feeling slightly helpless and vulnerable. This wasn't an unpleasant feeling though – I'm no psychotherapist but I imagine that somewhere in your unconscious mind it helps trigger off memories of when you really were a baby, a time when you had no responsibilities, no bills to pay and no concerns other than where your next meal was coming from. Being an adult baby may not necessarily be just about sex then, it could also be a form of escapism. And if that's what you need, then good luck to you – I can highly recommend it.

The thing about sex is there's really no accounting for taste, and it's no longer so easy to dismiss something like 'water-sports' or 'infantilism' as unacceptable or necessarily weird. What qualifies as one person's erotic turn-on is incomprehensible to another – we're all different. But what's certain is that fetishes – or 'paraphilia' to use the more correct term – however demented they may appear, are an undeniable part of the sexual fabric of modern life.

Paraphilia are essentially sexual impulses, urges and behaviours which deviate from accepted cultural norms. Research has shown that, for some reason, they are far more common in men (by about twenty to one) than in women. Many are considered highly morally dubious and, while they may get you off, they may also land you in jail. Certainly in the UK, you'll get yourself into trouble even if you indulge in some of the milder forms of paraphilia like exhibitionism (getting your todger out in front of strangers) or frotteurism (touching or rubbing yourself against a non-consenting person).

In the past, because of more stringent moral codes, the vast majority of sexual deviations were frowned upon. Masturbation for instance, although nowadays considered 'natural', was once, in certain cultures, nothing less than a huge taboo. Likewise, homosexuality was, in the past, considered way out of line – today however, it's thought of as just a bit niche. In fact, whether your sexual kink is deviant and illegal depends entirely on your cultural and historical context – in 21st century Britain you can have gay sex with a man of eighteen and if you later decide to get married then it's game on. But imagine doing that a hundred years ago. Or in Iran.

As I see it, yesterday's perversion is today's alternative lifestyle. It may even turn out to be tomorrow's accepted standard of behaviour. A simple change in the law to the age of consent, for example, means that overnight you can go from being guilty of a sex crime to practising an accepted form of love-making.

In terms of what's deemed acceptable or not, things are changing faster than ever before. Shucks, it's getting more and more difficult to offend anyone these days. You can pick up a daily tabloid newspaper and read about role-model celebrities indulging in orgies, dogging, spit-roasting and swinging parties. A Christmas party piss-up at a Premiership football club is no longer a playful night down the local nightclub, it's a gaggle of hand-picked women and hotel rooms hosting a series of gang bangs. Apparently.

Today, society is bombarded with sexually-loaded fetishist images – go out on a Friday night in most Western cities and the fashion of prostitutes is pretty much the prevailing style for clubbing girls – even teen idols like Britney Spears and Christina Aguilera borrow from the streets by wearing rubber dresses and thigh-high fuck-me stiletto boots in pop videos that have far more in common

76

with pornos than with children's television.

The new sexual permissiveness we see today owes itself to a great degree to the explosion of the Internet. Back when I was a young lad, you got your kicks by buying a porn mag – along with all the incumbent hassles and embarrassment. Today, a teenager with a personal computer can have access to the world's biggest porn collection in mere seconds. By having contact with increasingly titillating and explicit material, youngsters have become more familiarised with all manner of sexual variants. On the one hand I think that's a good thing – that what was once hidden and illicit is now more mainstream, more understandable. On the other hand, at the risk of sounding like a party-pooper, sex shouldn't be just another throwaway product or an amusing sport – it involves feelings as well as orgasms. I'm no saint myself, but I'd hate to think that love and romance should ever cease to become part of the mix.

With that in mind, I suppose it's fortunate that not all paraphilia have successfully nudged their way into mainstream culture and into the suburbs. Despite the ubiquity of sexual mores, some kinks are still hidden, and a few of them are mind-blowingly off the beaten track. Here's just ten of what I consider to be among the most bizarre:

Agalmatophilia: getting turned on by statues, mannequins, and dolls (the Japanese are big on this).

Coprophagia: consuming faeces, smearing doo dah on the body as part of sexual play.

Apotemnophilia: gaining sexual pleasure from seeing a healthy limb, digit (or even the genitals) getting amputated.

Spectrophilia (also known as amaurophilia): imagined sexual arousal by spirits, ghosts, angels and other spooks.

Emetophilia: being turned on by vomiting or by seeing others throwing up.

Eproctophilia: if you get a stiffy after farting, smelling and or hearing other people float one, then eproctophilia is your thing.

Crush fetish: seeing small creatures or insects being crushed by members of the opposite sex – or being crushed yourself.

Gynophagia: gaining pleasure from the idea of eating women.

Plushophilia: fantasizing about people wearing furry animal costumes (how did I never get laid as News Bunny then?).

Dendrophilia: kinky nature lovers getting turned on by an extreme form of tree-hugging, i.e. having sex with them.

Don't worry; all of the above will be covered at length in the next series of *Sin Cities*. NOT. Joking aside, I think as long as your kink is consensual and doesn't harm anyone else, then its fine by me – that's gynophagia out of the loop then. Seriously though, I'm reluctant to sneer at someone else's fetish and condemn it as 'wrong' or 'flawed'. It's not: it's just part of who you are. The more 'vanilla' or traditionally straight people tend to fall into the trap of thinking that their lack of self-knowledge means they have no deviant perversions – they probably do, they just haven't explored them yet. And that's where I enter the equation: my job was to road test all the sexual variants we could find, some of which we'd never even heard of. That's why I'd ended up pissing my pants in a nappy in South Africa and watching girls burst their banks in Australia – to enlighten, entertain and inform. You're welcome!

After the Wet Set shoot, the crew and I took a well-deserved rest – we had flown in from the Philippines just 48 hours earlier, hadn't slept a wink, and had negotiated our way through streams of piss to finally arrive back at the hotel. We were exhausted. Usually the hotels we stayed in were pretty basic – *Sin Cities* was filmed on the tightest of budgets – but in Sydney we were staying at Pier One, a classy hotel with a cracking view of the Harbour Bridge and Sydney Opera House. It was just what I needed after such a gruelling schedule. Although I was growing accustomed to our usual prison cell accommodation, this was a change I'd have no problem with. Australia rocked. It had everything I loved about life: great beaches, lovely weather, excellent nightlife, fantastic people, beautiful women, 24-hour casinos and plenty of sport on the telly... it ticked all the boxes for the perfect lifestyle. And now I could add the most comfortable bed in the world to the list as I felt myself drifting off, smiling and content to be able to close my eyes. And – bonus – it was about to get even better.

chapter 8
kylie and cindy

One of the best things about presenting *Sin Cities* was
that I often had to go and experience some of the most
erotic and sensual pleasures available to humanity. In
Sydney, we booked a day's filming at a renowned massage emporium, which catered specifically for couples
who, in a bid to spice up their sex lives, were treated to a
naked body-to-body massage. Because I was single, I
needed to get myself a date for the occasion, and seeing as
we were in Australia, Duncan decided that my date
should be a Kylie Minogue look-a-like. *Genius.*

After some hasty research, our very own Kylie arrived
in the lobby of the hotel. She was a fairly good likeness to
the real thing, and seemed amused by the idea of getting
a naked massage. We hopped into the car and I drove her
down to the location so we could get to know each other a
bit before the shoot. I liked her straight away – she was a
cool girl, up for a laugh and seemed like fun. I was feeling
a little flirtatious and 'Kylie', it seemed to me, was giving

as good as she got. She was one of those girls who you know, just as soon as you meet them, that they like you, the feeling's mutual... and sex is definitely on the cards. I don't mean to imply that I thought she was a tramp, but I pretty much knew that sooner or later we would end up shagging. Turns out it was sooner than I could possibly have hoped for.

As we arrived for our massage, we were immediately directed towards the showers. Oh I see, we were having a shower together were we? Fine by me. Kylie too had no issues with this, so we duly took up our first positions and stepped naked into the shower together. This was getting better and better. Kylie and I starting soaping each other down and it wasn't long before young Kylie had my cock in her hands. Mmm, lovely... 'I'm just gonna turn you around a second there Kylie.'

Kylie leant against the wall of the shower, bent over slightly and parted her legs invitingly. Duncan meanwhile was straining his arms in an increasingly ridiculous attempt to stick his camera over the partition and get some footage. As I pushed the lens out of our faces with one hand, with the other I was getting into my second position by gently easing my cock into Kylie. Soap suds dripped down her back and onto her pert bottom as I began to move in and out of her. She looked back at me approvingly and I felt like the cat that got the cream. Annoyingly, the distant cry from Duncan of 'Hurry up in there, we've got some fucking filming to do' pulled me swiftly out of my reverie: we'd have to hold that thought and carry on later.

We dried each other off and headed into the massage room, with Duncan looking on at me like a proud father upon his slightly wayward son. For the massage, Kylie and I stretched out naked on two tables placed side-by-side. At that moment, in walked two stunning blonde

Aussie girls, both completely naked and covered head to toe in baby oil. No sooner had I yelped with glee than one of them was lying on top of me slithering up and down with her naked breasts rubbing against my back. I looked over at Kylie who gazed across and winked at me. Had I died at that moment, it would have been the perfect ending. However, it wasn't yet my time to depart this planet and I felt the distinct ache of disappointment that life, from now on, was always going to be a downhill trajectory. And then, another sliding motion of the naked blonde on top of me as she moved up towards me and nuzzled my neck: maybe life was worth living after all. With her massaging me, I lay there watching a Kylie look-alike who I'd been bollock-deep in just moments ago with another naked girl writhing up and down her body. And I was on a promise.

I have to say, I didn't make a habit of having sex with the contributors of *Sin Cities*. One other notable exception, however, was Cindy – a girl who spent her days having virtual sex in an Internet booth in Hamburg. The instant I met her, I had the same connection.

We started filming Cindy early one afternoon. She was lying down on a makeshift bed dressed only in skimpy knickers and bra. She was in her early twenties, had long blonde hair, slender but curvaceous body, cute smile, and spoke in broken English: a winning combination by which she had me smitten at 'Guten Tag'. The format of Cindy's show, as you can probably guess, was quite simple and the only frill in terms of production values was her lingerie. The premise was that people would log on to her site and ask her to perform various tasks to help turn them on. Whatever they requested, from fondling her breasts to masturbating with dildos or talking dirty, Cindy would oblige. She showed me the sex toys that she used to titillate her viewers, and as I was eager to get inside her knickers, I was mindful not to take the piss out of the tools of her trade like I had done in my screen test that time.

After a quick interview she invited me to stay with her to help her perform for her viewers. She suggested I take my clothes off and lie down next to her. After a fraction of a second considering this fantastic offer, I did exactly that, only for Cindy to then request that I take off my boxer shorts so she could wear them.

'Fair enough,' I replied, 'let's swap underwear.'

When she took her knickers off, I immediately noticed that there was a distinct wet patch on them... what the fuck?! Never having shied away from the crunch question, I immediately asked, 'Have you pissed your pants or did you just forget to wipe?'

Cindy looked at me quizzically. 'No, you turn me on. I like you,' she replied. 'You make me wet just by looking at me.'

How often in your lifetime do you hear anyone say that to you? With those simple words, Cindy had just displaced Halle Berry from the top of my fantasy shag list. When we were done filming, I asked for her number and left her sex booth clutching my golden ticket, a smile on my face, promising to call her later on. But just several hours later, I thought I'd blown it – the *Sin Cities* crew and I had ended up going on a bender around town and I was steaming drunk. I was having way too much fun and it was now about four o'clock in the morning and I'd neglected to call Cindy. I know I said I'd call her later, but later was so late it had become early. And I was totally off my face! Then a voice in my head: 'You're going home tomorrow Ash, it's now or never. Call her!'

A tired Cindy answered the phone.

'Oh, hi Cindy, do you fancy coming round?'

Cool as a cucumber, Cindy asked where I was staying, said she'd be round before work and would I still be in my hotel room at eight o'clock? Bingo. Cindy duly arrived, a vision of blonde locks, pert boobs and lingerie. Dammit, I loved this job!

Sex with Cindy was not exactly mind-blowing but this was totally understandable – I suspected her job had left her somewhat fatigued by the physical act of love-making, and besides, maybe she was leaving something in reserve for her Internet clients. 'Hey Cindy, have a good day at work,' I said afterwards. Cindy smiled and left the room, a full eight-hour shift of dildo-bashing ahead of her.

chapter 9
the joy of pain

Back in Australia, after my all-too-brief fling with Kylie, things were moving swiftly on from pleasure to pain. We had heard about a so-called house of ill-repute over in Melbourne known as The Correction Centre, where the girls specialised in kidnap, trampling, and torture — perfect *Sin Cities* material.

I think it's relevant to reiterate that at this point, when I was still starting out on my *Sin Cities* tour of duty, my own sex life was what is known in the adult industry as 'vanilla' — in other words, I was not particularly adventurous in the sack. My preference was for swift, casual sex, usually in bed, invariably with one girl, without the use of any sex toys, and with the minimum of foreplay. Odd then, I'm sure you're thinking, that I should end up as a sex reporter, but there you go.

In terms of S&M, well, the honest truth is that I would have been hard pushed to know what those letters actually stood for. Besides, I'd always had a very low pain

85

threshold and didn't have any desire to feel pain or inflict pain during the pursuit of sexual satisfaction. I was after an orgasm, pure and simple, preferably with the minimum of fuss, the quicker the better. Pain, for me, was an entirely separate and distinct feeling to pleasure, and had no place in the bedroom.

The girls at The Correction Centre were determined to prove me wrong. As soon as I entered the place, they immediately showed me who was boss by throwing a leather hood over my head and shoving me to my knees. There were three of them, all dressed in red and white rubber nurse outfits, leaning over me and subjecting me to a torrent of verbal abuse. They were on a mission alright.

'Dickheads,' I muttered.

'What?!' They screamed back at me. 'What did you say?'

'Nothing,' I whimpered.

'Put a gag on him,' I heard the head nurse order her subordinates.

I was then gagged, had a dog collar and chain put around my neck and was led upstairs on all fours.

'Someone's been a naughty boy haven't they? Someone's going to be punished.'

'Oh really, who?' I chirped up from behind my gag.

'English idiot! Get up on the table. It's time you were dealt with once and for all!'

I'm sure that was racial abuse, but I had no time to enquire about abuse etiquette. My hood was lifted and there in front of me was a rack with chains and handcuffs at each corner and leather straps hanging ominously from the sides. I didn't like the look of this one bit. I looked around for Duncan – did he want me to get strapped up and tortured? I was getting worried. These women were clearly out to prove their point and looked deadly serious.

'What's up, Ash?' Duncan asked.

'What do you think?'

'Just do as they tell you. If it gets too painful, say "stop filming" and we'll stop and make sure you're OK. If you don't say those words then we'll carry on until you do.'

Duncan couldn't help smiling. He was loving this. He knew I was a cheeky little fucker and would be up for the challenge, and in a way I was. I had always been very cynical of the sado-masochistic scene and wanted to show it up for what I thought it was – just a load of goths hitting each other and persuading themselves that they were pushing the boundaries of sex and sexuality. They couldn't scare me with their mock prisoner of war torture chamber. Could they?

My big problem was that I was not a fan of getting hurt, and everything around me spelt pain. I'd already had my hair pulled, been slapped, kicked and dragged around on my hands and knees. And that was just the beginning. Oh well, better take the rough with the smooth if I was to do this properly. I got up on the rack and Nurse Betty, a slightly plump but foxy-looking Japanese girl, began strapping me down. So far, so good. Before long I was completely immobilised with my arms and legs tightly fastened. Then the girls really started to swing into action. Nurse Betty kicked things off by pinching my nipples, softly at first and then, gradually, with real venom. Out of sight, I could feel one of the others hitting the inside of my thighs with what turned out to be a studded paddle – basically a modified table tennis bat.

As Duncan recorded the action, I unwittingly began to up the ante by provoking the girls and putting up a fight. In between bouts of writhing around and trying to twist my body away from my kidnappers, I began shouting abuse back at them.

'Fuck off. That hurts, you bell-ends!'

Another hit: harder this time.

Nurse Betty bent over me, an evil smile on her face. 'What did you say? Idiot!'

I saw that she was holding something. What the fuck was it? Then I found out. Nipple clamps. Metal ones. Like clothes pegs. On my red-raw nipples. I took a sharp intake of breath as she let go of them. That hurt... that really fucking hurt. More tightly-sprung clothes pegs were attached to the inside of my thighs.

'What the fuck? That really fucking hurts!'

Even though I was being filmed, I was no longer aware of the camera and didn't care that we were here to make a show. This was too much. I wasn't built for pain. My inner-self was screaming, 'I'm a sex reporter. Get me out of here!' but part of me also wanted to beat these girls and show them that I could take it; that I was stronger than them and could handle whatever they could throw at me. *Come on then!* Another shot of the paddle to the soles of my feet had me screaming in agony. I struggled some more to loosen my bindings but they didn't shift. And then felt another blow to the stomach, this time with a whip.

'*Fuck!* Fuck off, man!' I gasped.

'I'm afraid you don't understand do you, young man?' came the reply. 'We're in charge here and we don't approve of swearing. We're going to have to gag you again.'

Nurse Betty stepped forward holding a new gag, this time in the shape of a small rounded penis. Even I had to respect the perfect humiliation of that – these girls were obviously true pros. Betty shoved it into my mouth and wrenched it tight. I was in a real mess here. Sweat began to drip down my face as I saw another of the girls reaching for the horse whip. She brought it crashing down onto the clothes pegs attached to my thighs. A stifled '*Fuck!*' escaped from between my gag.

'Are you still swearing? Oh dear, what a stupid little boy. Let's put a stop to that shall we. Each time I whip you, I want to hear a "thank you." If you fail, your punishment continues. Understand?'

I gurgled agreement. At this stage, my 'treatment' had been running for nearly an hour, during which time I had gone from fighting against the will of my torturers, to being fully submissive. This, I'd begun to understand, was the mental state – the psychological point where the girls wanted to take me. I'd been battered into submission, my ego smothered in pain and I had to face a horrible reality – if I didn't do and say exactly what they wanted, then more punishment was on the way. If I wanted out, I would have to comply.

Nurse Betty lifted the horse whip. I closed my eyes. She brought the whip down at speed, clipping the clothes pegs attached to my nipples. Searing pain followed.

'*Arrrgggghhhhhhh!*' And then, the now-compulsory 'Thank you.'

'Well done, Ashley. And again.'

No. No, no. NO! PLEASE NO! Twice more Nurse Betty brought down the whip and each time I forced out a muffled 'Thank you'. After what was probably the third or fourth blow, I had something of an epiphany. I was utterly consumed by pain, but suddenly, after all the agony and torture, I found myself somehow relaxing into it. I assumed that I'd probably crossed my pain threshold and was overcome by an incredible sense of relief. I was completely at their mercy but there was a difference: right then I simply didn't care. All I knew was that it couldn't get any worse than that.

I exhaled. Another blow to my tit ripped the clothes

peg off, sending blood rushing back into my squeezed nipple. Another on-rush of pain, and of course, a 'Thank you.' I was in such an intense state that, incredibly, the agony had somehow become something approaching... *ecstasy*. I relaxed again. More pain, more endorphins. I was elated. The final blow, the final gasping thank you, and it was over.

A tiny part of me wanted it to continue. That one-hour onslaught of punishment and torture had given me my first real insight into the hardcore world of sado-machocism. During those final few minutes, I was able to understand that pain and pleasure, in a very fucked-up and powerful way, can sometimes become interchange-able. Being fairly new to reporting in such a hands-on manner, I felt I'd definitely earned my stripes. What's more, I left The Correction Centre thinking that in the future I might, just might, add some spanking to my bedroom repertoire. I'd keep the clothes pegs for their intended use, though.

chapter 10
getting nailed

My belief in a happy relationship between pain and pleasure was to prove short-lived. A visit to New Zealand, and, specifically, to a tattoo parlour with a lucrative sideline in extreme piercing, was the first of many instances where pain was exactly what it says on the tin – fucking painful.

Having now taken on the official mantle of the *Sin Cities* guinea pig, I was to engage in this particular establishment's latest fad, namely the insertion of two large meat hooks in the back, which were then attached to a winch aimed at hoisting the victim off the floor. Note the word 'victim'.

Each hook was about half a centimetre thick – that may not sound a lot, but when it's ripping a hole through your flesh, it's plenty big enough. The first hook was inserted in at the top of my back and I was one unhappy little guinea pig. When the second one was pushed in and secured – and God, it hurt like fuck – I was hoping the agony was over. Sadly, it wasn't that easy. There was another stage yet to go. The hooks were attached to a hanging chain and the slightest movement was excruciating. Then the chain was pulled taut and I was left moaning in agony, and believe me, I moaned. I couldn't handle pain like that. It just wasn't natural to want someone to do that to you. As I pushed my body up on tip toe to avoid any more weight being borne by the hooks, I cried out for it to stop. I'd had enough.

Sin Cities, much to my displeasure, was morphing from a sex show into some kind of world of pain experience. When we looked back at the footage later on in the comfort of our hotel, it did appear that I somehow made a good victim. Duncan, who had a keen eye for comedy, was tickled by my suffering. He felt there was something about me which called out for me to be put to rights, that the infliction of severe discomfort somehow suited me. That's not to say that sex was no longer our number one priority: it was. But Duncan, ever the conscientious director, now always had half an eye on looking for ways to make me suffer. Several weeks later, he'd found his dream scenario.

The whole thing began as a germ of an idea in the back of a taxi in London during a week-long break from filming. Duncan looked across at me.

'Hey Ash,' he began. 'We've got a slight problem with the Paris show.'

'Oh yeah?'

'Yeah. It's looking a bit weak. We need to pep it up a bit.'

'Oh God. What do you want me to do?'

'Well, you don't have to... but there's a couple of things we're looking at.'

If this was a feature film, they'd probably have a grab-freeze frame at this point so you'd see my expression change from worried to petrified. After a couple of seconds, we'd be back to real time and Duncan would continue.

'Well, the first possibility is getting you to have a Prince Albert.'

And then you'd see the colour drain from my face as it registered. If you don't know, the Prince Albert is, for a man, an excruciating prospect. It involves piercing the end of the penis and then inserting a small metal ring. Supposedly, wearers enjoy a far more stimulating sex life due to the increased amount of exposed nerve endings. If he was softening me up with the good news, I needed to know the rest.

'The other thing we could do is pay a visit to a French dominatrix, Mistress Elsa, who does an extreme form of piercing through the scrotum.'

'Fucking hell, Duncan!'

'Listen Ash, you don't have to do either,' he reassured me. 'Both are going well beyond the call of duty, so...'

'Fuck it. Let's make this easy. I won't do both – it's too much. But I'll do one or the other. You're the director, you choose. Just promise not to make me look like too much of a cock and I'll go with whatever you want.'

'OK,' Duncan replied. We shook hands on it. 'We'll do the scrotum.'

Duncan was no mug. The Prince Albert, although severely painful, is nevertheless a fairly standard procedure. He knew this and knew that 'standard' wouldn't make good television. In Mistress Elsa, Duncan had found someone who delivered a truly unique service that would answer his brief.

Walking up to the door of where she worked in the centre of Paris, I was starting to feel panicky. I'd been dreading the moment ever since the original conversation in the taxi and actually standing outside the place made it all too real. Duncan, on the other hand, was visibly excited. During our last couple of months on the road we'd become good friends, but sometimes, let's face it, we like to see our friends suffer. I was under no illusion that today, for Duncan, was going to be a very good day.

In preparation for filming, he'd checked out Mistress Elsa's web site and noticed with glee that she specialised in numerous forms of cock-and-ball torture. As we'd discussed, this usually involved hammering nails into the nad-bag, but he'd also seen a picture of someone's cock which had been turned into a candle – a wick had been fed down the Jap's eye and set on fire until it extinguished itself against the burning flesh of the victim. I say victim, but bizarrely enough, the people who left Mistress Elsa's scarred for life, were in fact, paying customers. They pay up to $500 an hour for the, ahem, pleasure of having their privates mutilated.

Let's move away from Mistress Elsa for a moment and take a closer look at why people would want to have this done to them. As usual, where sex is concerned, I think there are no hard and fast answers. Maybe wanting someone to inflict torture and abuse on your body relates to some kind of psychological need to be submissive. If that's what the client wants – having his bollock-bag attacked and his knob end shredded with a cheese grater – then it takes that need to an extreme level. And the customer is always right.

But I'd also hazard an educated guess that this need to feel submissive and vulnerable actually reveals a deeper desire to connect with feelings of trust in another human being. When you are at the mercy of a dominatrix wielding a hammer and some nails, as I was soon to find out myself, what you are doing is essentially placing your health and safety in her hands – you are, after all, putting yourself in a position that could leave you physically maimed for life. It's the ultimate adrenaline rush in that case – the risk, the uncertainty that it will go too far. The dominatrix however, will only take you to the limits that you agree beforehand – a verbal contract, including a safety word so that the she knows when to back off and halt proceedings. It's a huge offering and something that, when you look at it, is a lot more complicated than just letting someone trash your testiculars until you have to shout your safety word (mine would be meringue) before you limp off home for a cold shower. The dominatrix never breaks that bond; she will never cross the line. In that respect, there is always an element of, dare I say, safety. The fact, then, that she will never betray that trust allows you, for a moment at least, to reaffirm your faith and trust in people. Although an unusual one, it is still her job, and her clients are the ones she needs in order to live.

On a more basic level, sometimes a little pain inflicted on the body can be nice. I'm not a major fan myself but I can appreciate that – a bit like in the film *Fight Club* – pain takes you out of your comfort zone, makes you feel more alive, real, vital. Not to mention an instant hit of endorphins to enliven an otherwise grey day.

I don't believe this is the motivation for all such clients – each and every one will have his own particular psychosexual kink and unique reason for putting himself in such an extraordinary position. All this may, to the uninitiated, seem a bit demented, even tragic, but I believe the paying S&M customer has successfully identified a need within himself. If a dominatrix helps him satisfy that need, then all power to his elbow.

Let me take you forward a few years to explain further, specifically to San Francisco and one of my most memorable encounters on the *Sin Cities* road. There I was to meet a client with the unlikely name of Mucus; a well-connected chap to say the least. Mucus enjoyed nothing more than to have his plums pummelled... so much so that he'd gone as far as buying a pair of frighteningly sharp stilettos for his chosen dominatrix – the charismatic Mistress Vinyl – for this exact purpose.

A tall, dark, and daunting figure, Mistress Vinyl appeared to revel in delivering exactly what Mucus wanted – namely getting his todger and tits spiked with her sparkling new red stiletto heels. When I asked Mucus what he actually did for a living, it turned out he was a highly successful professional and would otherwise be considered an upstanding member of society. In what amounts to something of the Jekyll-and-Hyde syndrome, for someone like Mucus, cock-and-ball torture allowed him to spend time on the opposite end of the power spectrum, to be ordered about, to be told what to do, to be punished and treated like shit. These were all elements he presumably felt were missing in his all-too-successful work life.

I don't think it's any coincidence that a high proportion of paying customers tend to be from the upper reaches of society, often with highly powered jobs. For Mucus and thousands of others like him, the dominatrix helps him to fill a vacuum and find a balance in life. I'd liken it to the physical equivalent of having a decent argument – it helps you clear the air, to regain tranquillity.

As a married man, someone like Mucus would also have perhaps been uncomfortable at the prospect of asking his wife to perform these functions for fear that she would ridicule him, or worse, reject him as a freak or a pervert. His relationship with the dominatrix, despite her performing an incredibly intimate and private service, is purely business, nothing personal. More importantly, and in probably a very different way from his relationship with his wife, it is also entirely non-judgemental.

I can try, but I'm not sure my own experiences fully qualify me to accurately explain the emotional needs of the paying customer. Rather than indulging in too much cod psychology, it's probably worth you hearing from someone in the know – namely, young Mucus's skilled torturer Mistress Vinyl. I got back in touch with her recently and asked her some questions about her profession.

Ashley: What do you think motivates people to pay others like yourself to inflict pain on them?

Mistress Vinyl: I think that people would pay to have pain inflicted on them if they haven't been successful in their private pursuit of these activities. I also believe that a paid service is sought out after non-paying encounters lacked something that professionals *can* provide, namely amazing beauty, fabulously equipped spaces and flexible scheduling without any strings attached. A trained professional is highly skilled and understands the needs of someone who is seeking BDSM. It just makes sense to see a professional for a positive outcome when one is seeking a painful encounter.

Me: What do you think the client gets from the experience?

Her: I think the client gets a non-judgmental situation without any strings attached. He doesn't have to worry about what this woman thinks of him, or whether she sees him as a freak. He doesn't have to wake up next to her the next morning and have her snigger under her breath about him playing like a piggy amongst a collection of shoes. He can show up at a date and time he chooses, experience his kink in a safe, clean, environment that is a true fantasy setting and he can then exit back into the outside world and resume his life as usual.

Me: What kinds of people come and see you and why do you think they need you?

Her: My clients consist of intelligent individuals who find the kink portion of their life is lacking. They are usually highly successful men who have achieved a distinct modicum of success in their lives and are seeking to explore their fantasies with someone who they consider an intellectual peer. I believe they need me because they don't have any other outlet for their kink. Since most of them are in committed relationships, they don't want to jeopardize that situation by revealing this side of themselves. By seeing me, they can keep that portion of their life hidden and only reveal it to me.

Me: What do you get out of it besides the money?

Her: Professional Domination lets me experience something new with each and every session. I abhor a daily routine and I enjoy the flexible aspect of this work. I never know who is going to be contacting me for future appointments, what they will be into, or how the various appointments will manifest themselves. I feel like I am producing mini acts of theatre each and every time I walk through the doors to the dungeon. My goal is for a standing ovation with each conclusion, but I'm aware that doesn't always happen.

Me: If you weren't being paid for it, is this something you would still want to you?

Her: I practised S&M long before turning pro and I will continue to do it when I'm no longer accepting payment. My kink is a part of who I am and not just my professional identity.

Me: What are the services you offer?
Her: I cater to couples and individuals who have an understanding of their kink and want to further pursue bondage and confinement, corporal discipline (whipping, spanking, strapping, etc), humiliation (verbal and physical acts), nipple torture, genital torture, cross-dressing and feminisation, tickling, trampling, fetish object adoration (shoes, gloves, boots, etc.), foot and leg worship, smoking fetish and cigarette torture, role-playing, piercing and cutting, and objectification.

Me: [Gulp] Can you give me an idea of the more bizarre/extreme requests you have received from your customers?
Her: I've had many requests over the years for bizarre activities, but the one that is currently at the forefront of my mind is when a client asked if I would nail his scrotum to a wooden box that I have. That ranks up there with some of the more bizarre/extreme activities I've ever done. Of course, cutting my logo onto someone's chest wasn't too shabby either!

Me: Quite. How does the role of a dominatrix differ from someone who is paid for sex?
Her: I like to think of a dominatrix as doing every-thing *but* having sex, and escorts as *only* having sex. A dominatrix will participate in a complicated role-playing scenario that sometimes lasts for hours. An escort sees you for penetrative sex of some sort, and

that's it. Complexity is at the heart of a professional session. Simplicity is at the core of a paid sexual service. This is how I see the difference between the two situations. A man seeing a dominatrix wants to ultimately engage his brain as a sexual organ, whereas a man seeing an escort only wants to engage the thing between his legs.

Good answer.

Me: If that's the case, then what role does sex actually play in the services you offer?
Her: If you are referring to oral sex or intercourse, those activities don't play a role in my services – at least from the standpoint of the client having sex with *me*. One of the justifications that many of my clients have for seeing me, even though they are married, is that we are *not* having sex and thus he isn't technically 'cheating.'

Me: Many people think what goes on in dungeons such as yours is just plain weird, perverted or even plain disgusting. I thought it was... funny and intriguing. How do you see it?
Her: I see what goes on in dungeons as fascinating. Yes, at times I have found extreme humour in what I just did to someone, but I don't see anything wrong with that. I guess I find it more bizarre when two men go into a ring and consensually beat themselves into unconsciousness than when I step on a man's head and he groans in pleasure.

So there you have it. Bizarre or otherwise, whatever you think, most clients return to Mistress Vinyl again and again because they believe it's money well spent. In

Mistress Vinyl's case, it was money that she ploughed back into her business, building a fully equipped dungeon with all manner of torture devices.

I find it a bit of a downer that she says a number of her clients visit because they are more comfortable revealing their kinks to a dominatrix – someone they may have found through a random Internet search – than to the partner who shares their bed every night. It's sad to think we are so fearful of rejection and our own partners mocking us. And even in the more permissive atmosphere of sex in the noughties, we run the risk of getting booted out of bed if we stray beyond the boundaries of what is considered 'normal'.

Sexual protocol is endemic in even the most progressive societies – if we find ourselves harbouring desires that we suspect would create conflict, the temptation is to keep them hidden. But letting that kink find expression at the hands of a dominatrix is important. By repressing it, the client could end up expressing his frustration in other ways and perhaps as a result jeopardise his relationship. So in a way, the conclusion I'm reaching is that a dominatrix like Mistress Vinyl is providing services that are essential for keeping the client healthy and settled rather than endlessly distracted and dissatisfied.

It was also a bit strange for me to hear, for the first time, that Mistress Vinyl had also indulged in a spot of scrotal nailing... which seamlessly brings us back to Paris and my encounter with Mistress Elsa. Here we can substitute the more glamorous red stilettos of Mistress Vinyl for the tools of a simple layman – one hammer and a box of nails.

I remember being so terrified at the prospect of what lay in store for me and my ball-bag as I rang the doorbell, that when the door opened, I flinched as Mistress Elsa

101

offered her hand to greet me. I knew it was going to be a particularly gruesome ordeal but Mistress Elsa quickly charmed me into adopting a more relaxed state of mind. She was a very glamorous-looking girl in her early thirties with long, dark hair and a seductive French accent. As she led me upstairs to her flat, I was suddenly aware of a man, naked except for a leather face mask, cowering in the corner of the stairway.

'Who's that?' I asked.

'He's a banker, works in the city. This is where he spends his holidays. Don't speak to him though,' she warned. 'He pays me to treat him like shit. In fact, he actually eats my shit.'

'He eats your shit?!'

Mistress Elsa nodded and led me into her kitchen. Then she opened up her fridge freezer and took out a plastic container.

'My shit,' she said matter-of-factly, lifting off the top. And there, unmistakably, lay the faeces of Mistress Elsa.

'I scoop it up and feed it to him as ice cream. It looks like chocolate, no?'

I had yet to come across sweetcorn and carrot-flavoured chocolate, but hey, there's always a first. My tour then continued into the bathroom, which had been specially converted into a 'scat room' – in other words, a place dedicated for poo-play. A bottomless toilet had been secured over the bath so that Mistress Elsa could take a dump on top of any customer keen to have a fresh dollop of turd land on them. This girl, truly, was different class.

The next door opened up to what was to be my home for the next couple of hours – a gleaming white medical room. She explained that my operation was to take place on a small horizontal couch. Everything was sterilised, my health would not be at risk and there would be no permanent damage. I was told to strip naked while she put on a change of clothes... Mistress Elsa would be back in a couple of minutes. Dread welled up in me.

As I sat on the couch to undress, I looked down and saw that beside me was a small bowl – in it were seven or eight nails, swimming around in disinfectant. Then, fully naked, I sat for a minute, my legs swinging in the air as I contemplated my horrible future. I felt like a condemned man. Mistress Elsa entered the room, a vision of sultry French sauciness decked out in a rubber nurse's outfit, and snapped me out of my darkened mood in an instant. What a minx! I was starting to feel better already!

'Madame!'

'Are you ready?' she asked.

Mistress Elsa, whose gaping bosom would surely have persuaded the most devout Christian to renounce God and embrace the devil, motioned me onto the couch. Deep breaths, Ash. And then she placed the piece of wood on top of me, took hold of my sack and pulled it through the hole. Here we fucking well go. Stretching it out until the skin was taught, she held the nail down in place between her thumb and forefinger, and drew the hammer back, ready to pound the nail through and pin it to the wood.

'No, no, no. Stop! Hang on... wait!' I stammered. 'I need to... to get ready.'

Oh Christ! This was going to hurt so fucking bad. I had to get my head together. How do you prepare for this? Anyone? She was poised, focused... the room was deadly silent with anticipation...

'Aaaaarrgh!' I blurted out.

'But I haven't even started yet,' Mistress Elsa said, looking down at me with a less-than-reassuring smile. And then she did start. Did she ever! She brought the hammer crashing down onto the tip of the nail and sent it splicing violently through the skin. *Jesus-fucking-Christ.* I cannot *begin* to tell you the pain I felt. I hadn't

103

screamed like that since I was a baby. If I screamed when she just put the nail in place, imagine the sound I made as she hammered it through my scrotum.

Mistress Elsa looked at me, alarmed. 'What's wrong?' she asked.

'What's wrong?! What do you think is wrong?! That fucking kills!'

'This was not pain. This is easy,' she insisted.

'It's not easy. This is something very fucking far from easy!'

'We'll do the second nail now. That will be better.'

She may have had a cracking set of breasts on her, but that didn't matter after the first nail. And the second nail was not better. In fact, it was a whole lot worse. Now that I knew how painful the first insertion had been, the prospect of the second nail was enough to set me right on edge. I writhed around, agonising at the thought of another brutal blow.

In the background I could now hear the uncontrolled giggling of Denise, our young Italian assistant producer. I almost forgot they were in the room with all the excitement going on. Both she and Duncan, as predicted, were loving it. I couldn't blame them. In fact, hearing them laugh gave me the encouragement I needed to go on: as long as it made people laugh, then at least something positive could come out of it. Scant consolation, but still – I was clutching at straws. As Mistress Elsa reached for the hammer I began to seriously doubt if I could go through with this.

'No. Please, no. I don't think I can do this.'

Mistress Elsa, much to my pleasant surprise began stroking my chest and whispering encouragement to me.

'There, there. It's OK. You see, with the pain, I now give you some pleasure.'

She looked gorgeous and despite the discomfort I was

under and the distress she had caused me, I could no longer resist.

'Can you show me your tits then, please?'

I was half-expecting a slap in the face. Instead, Mistress Elsa moved towards me, leant over and lowered her top, leaving her breasts resting gently on my face. The feel of soft skin, the smell of a woman – it hits the mark every time. I got what I wanted and I was immediately reinvigorated and prepared myself for the second nail.

One tap of metal on metal. More screaming. Another tap, stronger this time, but no less painful, as the head of the hammer slipped off the top of the nail and crashed directly onto my ball sack.

'FFFUUCCKKK! You just hit my fucking bollocks! What the fuck?!'

'Sorry. My mistake.'

'Be careful, please,' I begged her. 'These are my bollocks we're talking about here!'

Mistress Elsa took aim again, and fired. A clean hit. The nail had now gone through my sack and it was firmly lodged into place. I was screaming, shouting, then groaning.

'Oh my God, oh my God, that fucking hurt. Duncan, Dunc, I can't take it anymore. Please. I can't handle the pain. Stop filming.'

In the many months I was to spend with Duncan and the hundreds of hours of filming that we did, I was only to utter those last two words on this single occasion. We always agreed to film anything and everything, no matter what state I was in, unless I specifically asked for the cameras to be switched off. 'Stop filming' was, in a manner of speaking, our own form of safety word and upon hearing it, Duncan put the camera down and looked over at me. He knew it must be bad if I told him to stop.

105

'Fuck, Ash, are you OK?'

'I don't think I can do this. It's too much.'

'It looks pretty intense' he admitted. 'But it's brilliant stuff. Are you sure you want to end it now?'

I wasn't budging. 'I'm done,' I said. 'Seriously, it's too painful.'

Denise, who had so far proved to be an awesomely entertaining companion as well as a semi-decent AP, came over to take a closer inspection of the work in progress... a mutilated scrotal sack and the owner, like a trapped animal, with nails through his nads, close to tears.

'Oh my god, Ashley, that's fucking hilarious. This is so funny! Are you OK though?'

'Denise, you nutcase! Do I look OK?!'

I was also feeling flushed, with beads of sweat dripping off my forehead and my breathing was laboured. The pain was far worse than I could possibly have imagined; I was way beyond my comfort zone.

Mistress Elsa now joined in the discussion. 'Yes, he seems in a lot of pain. But it's a shame. Two nails do not look good. Three nails would be a lot better.'

She inspected her work and began to explain that my ball sack was stretched and secured at two points – at quarter past and half past the hour. If we put a third nail in at a quarter to the hour, then it would have a symmetrical look and would therefore be far more aesthetically pleasing. This was unreal. There she was discussing my bollocks like she was Alan fucking Yentob. Aesthetically pleasing? Duncan couldn't resist commenting either.

'Ash, she's right, you know. If we did a third nail, it would look a lot better. Like a triangle.'

I thought for a moment. Just one more. 'You really think it will look that much better?'

Duncan smiled a winning smile. 'Just do one more nail

and then I'll tilt the camera up to your face and you can wrap the show up there and then.'

'Fuck it,' I said. 'Let's do it.'

'Brilliant. OK, hang on a sec.'

Roll to record. The moment of crisis had passed. Mistress Elsa happily picked up the third and final nail and placed it at quarter to the hour. Now I say crisis over, but it was merely a short respite before the delivery of the sharpest, most brutally intense moment of pain I have ever, and hopefully will ever experience. *BANG!* The nail shot through me in one agonising flash. The mother of all screams... the intensity... the rush of blood... the camera tracking up my body to frame my agonised face in close up. Christ, what could I say? Words tumbled out:

'Well, that's all from Sin Cities in Paris... where my balls are... oh God, they're all over the shop!'

And that pretty much summed up the state of my gonads. I was scared to look. The Hames family jewels were stretched out in a star shape on a wooden base, secured at three points by the nails. Mistress Elsa stood back from her subject, beaming. It was a proud moment for her as she proclaimed it a triumph. At least one of us was happy. I was delighted my agonising ordeal was now over and implored her to remove the nails. After admiring her work for one last time, Mistress Elsa grabbed a pair of pliers and began tugging at the nails. This in itself was not exactly a pleasurable experience, but I could put up with it, knowing that it would put an end to the pain and discomfort. Then I was freed! I gingerly got up from the couch and left the medical room to take a piss and check there was no leakage. Everything was sound on that front and I had been assured that my sex life would not be affected by my nailing – the holes where my chods had been impaled were mere flesh wounds and would heal within a day or two. As for the direct hammer hit to the

107

balls, those fellas were still a bit sensitive for a few more days and, if they could talk, would have taken a while longer to forgive me. We soldiered on.

After retiring to the lounge, I sat down and breathed a huge sigh of relief. Mistress Elsa sparked up a joint. Had she been stoned while performing her operation on me? That would certainly help to explain the faulty aim on the second nail... I looked at her and knew that this had been one of the most momentous days of my life. I had never been through anything quite so intense, and yet for her it had been just another day at the office. I was well aware that in her work, Mistress Elsa had done some of the most mind-bending sexual operations – way more gruesome, painful and extreme than what I had just suffered. What I didn't know was the true extent of some of the mutilations she had carried out.

'So what's the most extreme thing anyone has ever asked you to do?' I asked.

She looked at me and took a long toke on her spliff. She then proceeded to tell me about a man who had come to see her a few months before with a most particular request. She led the gentleman into her medical room, instructed him to stand up against the wall naked, took out a razor blade, sliced through his bollock-bag and then took them out. The man's balls, which remained attached by the narrow tubes that are wrapped up within the scrotum, were then lifted up to his face as they lay on the outstretched hands of his mistress so that he could see them in their full, bloody glory. How fucking mental is that?! After the lucky fellow had feasted his eyes on his own plums, Mistress Elsa then tucked them back into his sack and sewed him back up. *Holy Maloney!* It looked as though I had got away lightly.

I have no idea what would compel you to pay good money for something like that: Was he sitting at home one day thinking, 'Hmm, I'm kind of tempted to go along to Mistress Elsa later and, er, yeah, I think I'll get her to slice my knacker-sack open, pull my plums out and dangle them in front of my face. Oh, and then put them back in, stuff all the veins back and stitch me up again.'

Why? is the obvious question. Is that a sexual thing? Cock-and-ball torture is a recognised paraphilia, which goes under the heading of 'phalloorchoalgolagnia'. But who cares if it's got a label? What this man had had done to him was so disturbed that I really don't quite know what I think. It seems a bit wrong to say the least. But I guess some people are just less satisfied with the day-to-day norms of the average sex life – they feel restless and crave more excitement and stimulation. But this guy must have been seriously off his rocker! It's one thing to want to stretch your own boundaries, challenge yourself, to seek out something new, something more intense – but quite another to voluntarily pay for your own bollocks to be brutalised.

I'm also curious about what Mistress Elsa thought, when he came in and explained his request. I mean, what the hell does that make her think of men? I imagine she probably steers clear from analysing it too much – that way, madness surely lies. She's providing a service and perhaps even likes the stimulation of a new and exciting challenge. So in a way, both Mistress Elsa and her subject are getting the same thing out of the experience: a fresh challenge, a new insight.

I think perhaps they are also appreciating the thrill of finding something to shock themselves out of their everyday existence. Life can be pretty dull for many of us. Sex is a way of escaping that, which could be one of the many reasons it's such an obsession for so many people. Just like in a game of poker where no one hand is ever repeated, every single time you have sex it will inevitably be different. Sex can be spiced up in an unlimited manner of ways – for some that involves cross-dressing, for others it might be by talking dirty; but for this anonymous man from Mistress Elsa's client list, it meant exposing his gonads to the open air, tipping his hat and greeting them with a friendly 'Bonjour'.

Mistress Elsa was a true pro and I remember her with a real sense of affection. It's odd, I suppose, that after such a vicious operation, I don't feel any animosity towards her – quite the opposite. What I have found is that you can very quickly develop the sense of having a very strong link, the feeling of a shared and significant experience with a dominatrix – it becomes a precious moment, like you've both climbed a mountain together. It was clear, though, that while my own genital operation had been Mount Everest for me, for Mistress Elsa it was akin to walking to the shops. If slicing someone open and juggling his balls was part of her repertoire, then banging in a few nails must have been mere child's play. Despite this, she was, at the time, very sensitive to the significance of what I had been through. It was like a spiritual journey.

'Ashley, you will see and do many things on your travels, but this will stay with you forever. You will never forget this day. You understand this don't you?'

I did. For me, never had a truer word been spoken.

chapter 11
arse action

Mine were not the only pair of bollocks to receive a severe seeing to on the *Sin Cities* road. A few years later, and newly teamed up with a fantastic new director with the fantastic name of Paddy Ruddy, I was privileged to attend the session of a young German lad who appeared to be on a mission to outdo my own particular gonadic accomplishments.

Paddy and I were greeted with the most astonishing of sights: Thomas splayed out with his legs in the air on a gynaecological chair in a flat in Berlin. He was completely naked, save for a rubber mask from which he could just about manage to communicate with the woman standing over him – Mistress Silvia. Yes, I know, it sounds like a gag from a bad comedy routine.

While briefing me earlier about Mistress Silvia, Paddy warned me that she was quite a notorious figure around town. Mistress Silvia, to be clear, was not your regular dominatrix... not that I'm sure I've ever met a regular one. A tall, imposing figure, decked out in leather, with high heels and scraped-back dark hair, Mistress Silvia had been a professional dominatrix for over thirteen years, and described herself as 'cruel but caring'. Her repertoire was expansive: it included bondage, anal and toilet training, corporal punishment, humiliation, imprisonment, interrogation, nipple torture, breath control (including face-sitting and suffocation) electric stimulation, foot worship and pet-play (including dog training, pony training, hog feeding and slaughtering). That, I'm sure you'll agree, is a pretty impressive and extreme CV. Thomas was a regular client of hers, and one of his particular fetishes involved him getting his scrotum inflated with saline. Please don't ask why: thinking back on this time is making me feel far too weak to explain. Read on, and you'll understand.

When we arrived for filming, Thomas was already hooked up to a drip, which was infusing saline via a needle inserted into his gonads at a slow but steady rate in order to help increase the size of his genitalia. Mistress Silvia explained that the ball bags could stretch to huge proportions without any lasting damage, and she was aiming to expand Thomas's to the size of a coconut. Lucky lad.

After my treatment at the hands of Mistress Elsa, I was all too happy to take a back seat and enjoy watching Thomas suffer. Strangely though, Thomas didn't actually seem to be in any discomfort. Quite the contrary: despite the fact that his knackers had been pierced and was now approaching the dimensions of an orange, he said he was feeling extremely happy with the procedure.

I noticed, however, that Thomas didn't appear sexually aroused throughout his operation, so I asked him if he was OK.

'Yes, I love this,' he replied. 'I like to do anything that

pleases my mistress.'

And for him, it was clear, that was an essential part of the heady mix – Thomas was not just realising his own fantasies but felt he was also helping to please his mistress. Again though, why should anyone want to sacrifice his own physical comfort at the behest of someone for whose time he was paying? The relationship between client and dominatrix is complicated to say the least. I have heard many clients refer to their 'love' for their mistress, and Thomas, too, appeared to harbour a genuine affection for Mistress Silvia, as well as a deep affection for something else. As I walked around him to get a better look at how his scrotum was holding up, I couldn't help but notice that his freshly shaven backside appeared... well, let's just say it was immediately obvious that Thomas had recently had something up his bottom. I asked Mistress Silvia about my new discovery, and she instantly revealed that anal-play was one of Thomas's favourite hobbies. Sometimes the naughty schoolboy in me comes out and I can't resist pushing things a little further, just to see. This, my friends, was one of those times.

'Well, feel free to indulge him,' I suggested.

Mistress Silvia needed very little encouragement. Very soon the rubber gloves were on and one of her fingers was deftly inserted up Thomas's back door. I looked up at my masked friend who began moaning in pleasure. I knew in Thomas I had found an accomplice all too willing to indulge my own particular sadistic mischief.

'Mistress Silvia,' I started, 'I'm not sure the one finger's enough, perhaps you'd like to double up there.'

Mistress Silvia took my suggestion on board – one finger became two, two became three... I felt a little queasy at that point. I looked over at Mistress Silvia who was starting to get really stuck into the programme.

'We can do some fisting if you like,' she said.

And before I even had time to respond, she had pulled her fingers together and was now pushing all four of them vigorously in and out of Thomas. Crikey. As the saline continued to drip down into his bulging ball bag, a full fist was now pumping in and out of his hoop. Oh. My. God. This was starting to get disturbing. I'd heard about fisting, mainly popular within the gay community, but I had never actually witnessed it at, er, first-hand, so to speak. Out of everything that I had ever witnessed and experienced on the *Sin Cities* road, this was one of the very few times when I actually started to feel sick. I turned away from the action and physically retched.

When I looked back, Mistress Silvia still burrowing away and Thomas meanwhile, was groaning in ecstasy. I was wondering if my antipathy towards his anal fixation was revealing some kind of inner homophobia. I'm not sure that's the case, but certainly in my own sex life, I was never too keen on my bottom being brought into play. I've got my brown wings in a heterosexual context, but was never a huge fan. I'm pretty much a believer that the butt makes for a better exit-hole than an entrance. Mistress Silvia really gave his poop-chute a full-on pounding. Stopping for a moment, she picked up a small rubber sphere, attached it to a hand pump, and then inserted it up his gaping hole.

'We now see how much he can take of this,' she said, clenching her fists and pumping air to inflate the rubber ball inside him. After squeezing it about six or seven times she stopped. Thomas, she felt, had had enough.

'Go on, give him another, he's loving it,' I cried out, by now rather enjoying the fact that we were so obviously giving Thomas a great deal of pleasure. 'You are alright there aren't you, Thomas?' I asked.

'Oooh yes. Aaaah. Ooooh. Very much. Mmmm. I like,'

he stuttered in his thick German accent.

Mistress Silvia gave him two more pumps.

'By now', she said, 'the ball will be quite large, like an apple. It is probably best to stop.'

The word 'probably' was enough to seed some doubt in my mind – I grabbed the pump and squeezed it a couple of times. And once more, for luck. I was starting to giggle uncontrollably. Mistress Silvia, meanwhile, gave me a look suggesting it would be wise to let go of her instrument before Thomas's arsehole reached bursting point. I couldn't resist though, and gave it one final burst of air. Not wanting to live with the ignominy of having delivered lasting damage to another man's anal sphincter, I handed back the instrument to its rightful owner. Mistress Silvia deflated the ball to what I suspect was, by then, the grateful relief of Thomas.

Once it was successfully removed, she gave the ball the ten pumps of air that together we had just delivered to show us what size it had reached inside him. Thomas, it appeared, had been the proud recipient of what I reckoned to be an object amounting to the size of a large grapefruit. If I hadn't seen it – and been part of it – I wouldn't have believed it.

'We try the dildo now?' Mistress Silvia asked.

I was still stood in astonishment, but 'Too-fucking-right we try the dildo' came out my mouth before I could stop it. I turned to look at Thomas to check if that was OK for him. From the holes in his mask, his two eyes glinted with anticipated glee. Mistress Silvia left momentarily to return with the pièce de résistance – a large black dildo strapped to her crotch. Thomas, it seemed, was in for one hell of an afternoon. She positioned herself between his legs, deftly inserted the dildo inside him and then began... well, shagging the arse off him. Thomas gasped with pleasure as he took another hammering.

115

'You're loving this, aren't you sunshine?' I asked.

'Ja, it is very good. She is an excellent mistress.'

'I have to ask you this though, Thomas,' as Mistress Silvia continued rogering him, 'are you actually gay or not... because this seems, well, a bit gay to me?'

'No, I am not. I have a girlfriend. I just like it.'

And I suppose, in retrospect, there wasn't that much gaying up going on. Mistress Silvia, who continued to thrust expertly in and out of him, was female after all. Looking on, I started to feel a bit queasy again. This boy's arse got battered beyond all recognition – fingers, fist, rubber ball, and then eight inches of thick black dildo.

'Are you sure you're alright there, Thomas?'

A delighted Thomas looked up and smiled. 'Ja, ja,' he replied. 'Normally, I must pay for this!'

The fact that we had been there filming meant that Thomas had received the treat of a lifetime, free of charge. The *Sin Cities* team could be proud of themselves – we had just made one young man very happy indeed. 'Normally, I must pay for this' was soon to become a new catchphrase amongst the team whenever we enjoyed a freebie from the *Sin Cities* budget

'Free Internet access at the hotel? Hey, that's pretty good: normally, I must pay for this.'

'A drink on the house? Great! Normally, I must pay for this.'

And so on.

I think Thomas would have happily received another few hours of anal pummelling, but Mistress Silvia was keen to remove him from the saline drip. Already his arse had come close to breaking point and it looked like his gonads were ready to explode. After nearly two hours of saline fluid going into his Jacob's, it seemed that Thomas had achieved his goal... balls the size of a coconut.

Mistress Silvia extracted the needle and helped

Thomas up off the chair. It was an amazing sight. He stood up and between his legs was a set of barely recognisable genitalia, consisting of a hugely swollen scrotum, now so large that it pushed his penis up towards his stomach. Thomas though, was delighted, and more satisfied still that he had clearly pleased his mistress. She, in turn, looked back at him proudly as she inspected her work, satisfied with the job. Thomas, she revealed, would be the proud owner of his new elephant-sized scrotum for another seven or eight hours before the saline gradually dispersed. So everyone was happy! As for the arse, well, I suspected its recovery might have taken a little longer.

With Thomas, I had found the anal activity far more mind-blowing than the scrotal operation we had originally come to see. Thankfully my own rear end had escaped unscathed, and for that I was truly grateful. In fact, during the filming of *Sin Cities*, I had always given my directors very strict orders that, although I was cool with receiving fairly hardcore abuse from my dominatrix tormentors, the arse, it had to be understood, was strictly out of bounds.

I remember one of my directors, Aidan, bending my ear one day in Nice, France, where we had been having a bit of a battle to put a decent show together. Although we had filmed some dogging in the French countryside, a sex toy party and a night out in Cannes, we couldn't help thinking that the show was looking a bit lame, a bit standard. We needed some added pizzazz, some impact. Aidan, however, believed he had the solution to all our worries.

'Ash, as you know, we've been having a bit of trouble with the show...'

Already, this was starting to sound horribly familiar to

how Duncan had approached me about getting my bollocks nailed to a plank of wood.

'Tell me the plan Aidan, I'm all yours.'

'We've found a French dominatrix who will fuck you up the arse with a strap-on dildo. Are you cool with that?'

Oh, for fuck's sake.

'Am I cool with that?! Am I fuck! Please man, no anal penetration!! Come on Aidan, you know the rules!'

'Don't worry mate, you'll be fine!' Aidan broke out into laughter.

'Please Aidan, please mate… that means me getting buggered. It's sodomy. It's too much.'

'Do it as a favour. I promise I'll owe you one. Please. We'll make sure the strap-on is not too big.'

Aidan, it's fair to say, had been a great director and if anyone owed anyone anything, it was me to him. Although this was going well beyond the call of duty, I heard myself quietly agreeing to him.

'OK. I'll do it.'

'Good lad. Thanks Ash, you're a star. We're meeting her tomorrow afternoon.'

Comedy pause.

'Wave goodbye to that ring-piece, mate.'

And with that, he was off. The cheeky bastard. That night, it's safe to say, I did not sleep well. Later I woke up feeling extremely unhappy and was having some serious doubts about whether I could go through with this, but it was too late to back out now – everything had been arranged. We jumped in the cab and Denise passed me a sheet of paper with some research information and a picture of the lady who would soon be shafting me to hell and back. As I read about her, my hackles began to rise. I gazed down with tired and somewhat fearful eyes at a photo of her decked out in the obligatory black leather, brandishing a bullwhip. Soon enough, the car stopped at our pre-arranged meeting point and we sat back and waited.

After nearly an hour's wait, it was starting to look like I may have got off the hook. Our dominatrix, it turned out, was a no-show. Aidan and Denise had some increasingly frantic discussions, but numerous phone calls only revealed that Madame Strap-On was incommunicado. I was free to go back to the hotel with my back door intact and not a dildo in sight. Get in!

Aidan, however, was not a happy bunny and was understandably annoyed that Denise, who had set up the shoot, hadn't put a plan B in place. Because of the problems with the Nice show, of which this latest drama was a typical example of Gallic laissez-faire, we had all been under a lot of stress. Denise however, had the perfect solution. She suggested that to help us all chill out, relax, and get back on track, she would call up a couple of her Italian friends from just over the border and invite them over for a night out. Aidan and I agreed that we were due some fun and immediately passed Denise a mobile phone, warning her that if these girls likewise failed to show, then she, not me, would be the one with a dildo stuck up her arse.

Well, it turned out that Denise's friends were not the types to shy away from a rendezvous with a couple of English lads and the promise of some free booze and possible casual romance. In just two hours flat, they arrived at the hotel to find us. I speak fairly decent Italian, putting me in pulling pole position, and made good headway with the one of the girls, Nadia. Aidan however, could not speak a word of Italian, and the other Italian girl could, in turn, speak absolutely no English. Despite this, both Aidan and I managed to get ourselves well and truly laid that night. Not a bad effort on my part, but for Aidan, bearing in mind his conversation had,

119

by the end of the evening, merely progressed to saying a single word – 'ciao' – it was positively legendary.

I later asked Aidan how he had managed to communicate with his Italian lover after having sex with her.

'Well,' he explained. 'I didn't really. I just looked at her, smiled, and gave her the thumbs-up sign.'

Truly, the language of love is international. Denise, whose abilities at pimping had far outshone her skills as a producer, was forgiven everything. France, then, had not only seen me get shagged senseless by a hot Italian babe, but more significantly had seen a lucky escape for my butt. My 'No Back Passage' rule, and indeed my ring-piece, was still intact. But rules, as we know, are always there to be broken, and for me, this particular rule was thrown to the dogs while on a trip to Canada. I have many things to thank Canada for. This, however, was not one of them.

We arrived in Montreal in a similar situation to Nice – several shoots had fallen through and with only a week or so to do our filming, things were looking a bit dicey. At that time I was working with John, another director. John had been recommended for the job by his predecessor, Aidan. And while Aidan was a bit of a bad boy, even he was put in the shade by John, who, I soon discovered, was a hideous party animal. Oh well, at least the wrap party was guaranteed to be a mad one. A top lad, maybe, but let's not forget: we had some programmes to make here, and knowing John's reputation, it was difficult to trust him completely. And luckily I didn't.

Back in England, prior to departure and before we'd shot a single frame, we were loading up the van with all of our equipment. Just before we hopped in to head off to the airport, I thought it would be wise to double-check with John that we had everything.

'Are you sure you've got all the kit? I asked.

'No problems mate, it's all there,' came the confident reply.

I immediately felt like I had been a bit rude and patronising and should have shown a bit more faith in him.

Just to be sure though, I jokingly added, 'Camera? Batteries? Tape stock?'

'Oh fuck!' he said. 'Did anyone pick up any tapes?'

Shit. This was going to be a long couple of months! In fairness though, John had been brought in as director with virtually no time for preparation, so it was hardly his fault. The truth was that working under such crap budgets we were constantly rushing around at the last minute and taking short cuts to make the best of a bad job. John, it turned out, was a fine director, but more importantly, a great guy who was sometimes very, very funny. There were moments when he was so cheeky and unprofessional that I couldn't help but love him for it – he was *Sin Cities* through and through. Sadly, though, this didn't always make for the best results during filming.

I remember once, we arrived to film at a swingers' party, had a few beers and introduced ourselves to the scantily clad people that were there that evening. Then John asked me if I was ready to start – I would usually kick off with a piece to camera explaining where we were and, in this instance, explain who these writhing, naked bodies were behind me.

'Sure,' I said. 'Let's do it.'

John picked up his camera, held it in position, got it comfortable on his shoulder, and then, because I was in almost total darkness, flicked on the camera light. Without warning, this nearly blinded me. I just aimed my eye line to camera a few inches below the light, towards where I was hoping the lens was pointing.

I started my introduction; something along the lines of, 'Alright, so we've just arrived at a swingers' party – it's all going off behind me...' at which point I suddenly saw the light and camera lurch violently to the right. What the fuck was going on?! I leant over to see John with his head back, eyes closed in bliss, one hand still holding the camera and the other gripping a fresh bottle of lager to his lips! With John swigging away at his beer, the camera was pointing everywhere but in my direction. Even worse, he had no headphones on, so it was doubtful he could even hear a word I was saying! After catching my breath, I decided to indulge him for a minute and carried on with the introduction.

'No doubts about it,' I continued, 'things are getting steamy here. Maybe, just maybe, I'll get laid tonight.'

I stopped and then looked over at John. He placed the camera on the ground and took another satisfied swig of ale.

'Was that OK, John?'

'Sounded good to me, mate.'

'John! I love you, but fuck man! The camera was all over the place! I saw you necking that beer while you were filming me – you were all over the shop!'

'Nah, it'll be fine...'

I looked at him pleadingly.

'Mate, I'll show you the footage back, it'll be right as rain.'

With that, he re-wound the tape and sure enough, what he'd filmed what crystal clear, with scarcely a hint of a wobble.

'There you go, Ash. Have you never heard of steadicam? It's magic mate, magic!'

He certainly knew what he was doing. That said, and a couple of slightly iffy shoots later, we were having a bit of a nightmare trying to put a decent show together in

Montreal. What we needed was the same thing we had needed in Paris and then later in Nice – something to boost the show and give it a bit of a wow factor. Luckily, or rather, unluckily for me, we were to find it soon enough.

When we arrived at the house of Mistress Simone, in the suburban sprawl of Montreal, we had absolutely no idea what we would end up filming with her. Our planning was minimal – get in there, do a short interview, see where her talents lay and take it from there. If we weren't all seasoned professionals, we could have been accused of winging it. As the guys were setting up, I sat chatting to her to break the ice and put her at ease before being filmed. I couldn't help but notice there seemed something not quite right about her. For a while, I couldn't quite put my finger on it. But then, it became clear.

'Mistress Simone, I don't mean to pry,' I began. 'But were you actually born a woman?'

It turned out that my hunch was right. Mistress Simone used to be the far less glamorous Mister Simon but was now a pre-op transsexual. I had to hand it to him though – he did have a cracking set of knockers. But despite boasting a decent rack, my discovery that Mistress Simone was a she-male made me slightly more reluctant to do anything particularly intimate. That said, I was getting on pretty well with her/him (I'll plump for 'her' from now on – she'll appreciate that) and I was still aware that we were looking for something special to film, rather than any standard fare. Of course, when she revealed that she was a dab hand at performing enemas, John's eyes lit up.

'Yeah, Ash, let's get you an enema! Brilliant!'

Now, at the time, I didn't even know what an enema

was. I have told this story before and no one ever believes me, but I truly didn't have a Scooby Doo. So, not knowing what one was, I'd never had any interest in them nor had I ever felt the need to have one. Basically, without looking it up on the Internet, all I can tell you is that as far as I know, an enema is the flushing out of your insides by pumping water into your arse (that's unlikely to be the precise definition but it's pretty much what happens). Why Mistress Simone was a practised hand at this, I have absolutely no idea. Fair enough – you kick a ball, you find out you're good at football. How she'd originally discovered her knack for enemas was irrelevant at the time though... it was her forte, and much to my annoyance, that's what she was going to perform on me.

This being one of the many occasions when I was consciously sacrificing my own well-being and, indeed, dignity, I was determined to get at least some benefit out of it.

'How about we do it with alcohol rather than water?' I suggested optimistically. To my surprise, Mistress Simone claimed she had, in the past, done this very thing.

'We could use wine, if you like?' she replied.

Things were looking up.

'Have you got a decent bottle of red?' I ventured.

Mistress Simone promised to have a look and see what she could rustle up. I meanwhile, was directed into her medical room, a place which conjured up traumatic memories of my ordeal with Mistress Elsa. Surely nothing could be as bad as that? Well, put it this way, when Mistress Simone walked back into the room with a bottle of wine and a drip tube attached to a miniature dildo, I knew it wasn't exactly going to be a bed of roses.

Next on the agenda was for me to take off my clothes and lie on the bed face down in order to ease backdoor entry. I heard some giggling behind me, and I turned –

quite anxiously – to see Mistress Simone busy lubing up the nozzle that would soon be going up my back passage. The nozzle was shaped like a small penis. Oh Christ! John and Denise were by now shaking with laughter and completely incapable of holding their cameras steady. Whatever, you fuckers!

Primed and ready, or certainly as primed and ready as I would ever be, Mistress Simone put her nozzle into position... and then pushed.

'Ooooohhh!' I grunted. That was not a happy feeling. More pushing.

'You have a very tight arse,' she informed me. 'I need to push harder. Relax.'

Relax? Yeah right. I had to get up on all-fours and take it like a dog. More lube was administered, another push delivered, and fuck me ragged, it was in. Just to clarify, I was now in an apartment somewhere in Canada, face down on a bed, with a she-male shoving a cock-shaped nozzle up my poop-chute to give me a red wine enema. Don't you just hate it when that happens?

And Christ almighty! I mean, I don't have any issues with homosexuals, but you gotta tell me lads – how the fuck do you do it?! The object breaking my anal virginity was a mere fraction of the size of the average cock, and still it hurt like hell. And we're talking average size, flaccid.

I have to say it was pretty odd having my hoop stretched, but things became odder still when the tap was turned on and red wine began to flow. As I crouched there, I felt my entire arse begin to fill up with liquid. Denise, bless her, was grinning from ear to ear, having to stop herself from collapsing into laughter as she relished the look of hurt and distress on my face. The fact that any of her footage was actually usable was a small miracle, because every two minutes Denise would have to wipe tears of laughter from her eyes – this girl truly revelled in my suffering!

At times like these, I couldn't help but detach myself from what was actually happening to me and think how surreal and bizarre it must have appeared to anyone that would later be watching on television. Had I been seeing this on telly at home, I would have been thinking that this bloke, me, must have been off his rocker. And yet this *was* me – the same young lad who used to wear his little grey shorts playing conkers at prep school. Had this really been what my mum and dad had in mind for me to do when they dropped me off for my first day at university some ten years before?

Seeing Denise's face contorted with laughter set me off on a series of uncomfortable giggles, offset by the occasional influx of more wine. Annoyingly, the alcohol was now troubling my insides, coupled with the distinct burning sensation brought on by my anal invasion. I glimpsed behind me and saw Mistress Simone squeezing more wine down into the drip – it looked like I had already ingested well over half the bottle. Despite my suffering, I didn't object. Having gone that far, I was determined to get the entire load in – I always think that if you're gonna do something, then you may as go the full distance. I'd started so I'd finish. Besides, I like getting drunk, and I'd been assured that this novel method of consumption meant the alcohol would go straight into my bloodstream. Mistress Simone therefore instructed me to clench my cheeks together to stop the wine from dribbling out. Feeling exposed, lonely and somewhat vulnerable – but sadly, not yet inebriated – I did as I was told. It was no use, however. Despite my best efforts to hold my drink, as we approached the three-quarter bottle mark, I felt myself overflowing and screamed out that I was ready to explode. Mistress Simone sprang into action and pulled the plug. My bottom was freed, but my torment was far from over.

I ran to the toilet, collapsed onto the seat and readied myself for the shit of a lifetime. Now, I've had some curries in my time, but nothing could have prepared me for this. Cue Johnny Cash... ladies and gents, my ring felt like it was on fire. Wine sprayed the sides of the toilet and I pushed for England as I hurried to rid myself of my burning load. Stuff, and I think we can only really call it stuff, poured out in waves. After a painful struggle to eject the somewhat polluted vintage, it was all over, and I was left a slightly tragic and pitiful figure, sat dejectedly on a toilet seat in the house of a transsexual mistress, somewhere in the arse-end of Montreal. Red wine never again held the same appeal for me – from then on I was sticking to the beers, and no one, ever, was permitted anywhere near my rear-end again. And this time I fucking meant it.

chapter 12
single man, triple header

While that last incident was filed under the heading 'Never Again', Montreal was also home to one of the most amazing afternoons of my life.

One word, two syllables: blowjob. Most guys would probably agree that blowjobs provide them with their most memorable and enjoyable sexual experiences. Before my trip to Canada however, I would always have disputed this traditional male preference for the blowjob above and beyond the traditional shag. I'm not saying that I wasn't a fan – I was, am, and always will be – blowjobs are ace. They rule. It's just that sometimes they can get a little bit boring, quite quickly. This isn't because I haven't received my fair share of skilled blowers, I reckon I probably have. I think my lack of enthusiasm for oral sex stems from the fact that I've always found it quite hard to shoot my load from a blowjob, and for me, that's what sex is geared up for.

With this in mind, I arrived at the offices of a website

Thumbs up with the LIVE TV News Bunny.

Proudly sporting the News Bunny T-shirt before a home game of Topless Darts.

Filming (yet another pair of knockers) in Ibiza.

Another day in the L!VE TV orifice.

Topless Darts at the Circus.
A smash hit... with our several viewers.

If you find yourself
waiting for a drink
at the bar, then I
can highly recommend
doing this to help
pass the time.

Karaoke, Playboy style.

Jeannie is begging me to
take her to bed at this point,
but I insist we stay out drinking.

Smashed up and ready to film, somewhere in America. Probably.

Three absolute caners: Me, John & Denise. I look seriously ill and we've only just got started.

Mistress Vinyl commands Mucus
to bend over and take it like a
successful middle-aged
businessman with a wife and kids.

Adult babies
and their surrogate
mother in Australia.

Down boy! The incorrigible Felix
had just finished humping our assistant director.

Aidan and Kate in Hamburg -
we're about to go and film
the delightfully-moist Cindy.

Me and the main man,
John, in Kingston, Jamaica.

This photo is the only proof that I did
indeed have a night out in Rosarito, Mexico.
A lost night, but a night nonetheless.

I have no idea
where I was here
or what I was
doing, but I'm
pretty sure it was
a lot of fun.

No book is complete without
a large close-up shot of the
back of a cameraman's head.

Me and Kimber Lace
in LA: she had
just successfully
navigated her
way through
her first
girl-on-girl scene.

'Will you lick my asshole?' Daisy asks me.
Er, no.

The world's best pair of earings.

Duncan (director)
joins me, Daisy and Kimb[erly?]
for a heaven-sent
break in filming.

Denise and I
arrive at Montreal airport.
There appears to be
something up my nose.

On the set of (yet)
another porn shoot.

No, Ashley,
painting your
penis black
will NOT
make it
any bigger.

Me and Pricasso,
an artist
who paints
with his penis,
in Australia.

xtreme!
idan, me and Kate,
n our shocking
ight out in
Mavericks strip
joint in Cape Town,
South Africa.

Mia London.
And before you ask,
no I didn't.
Well, I might have done.
I like to keep things discreet.

Denise offers up some welcome refresh

Me and Taylor Wa

From left to right - Duncan (director), Dom (camera), Cat (producer),
Taylor Wane (porn star) and Laurien DuTremble (porn director)

Eat your heart out, Top Gear. Ceci gets the House of Gord makeover.

I'm starting to lose track of what 'normal' is.

And Gord said, 'Let there be light.'
And there was.

Ceci is winched up to form a human chande

Ibiza:
48 hours of AWOL
followed by a stint as a
Manumission girl.

A fresh but frisky
Lara James
before the orgy
onslaught in
Melbourne,
Australia.

Q. Who ate all the pies? A. Candy Godiva.

Rubber dolls:
even better t
the real thi
Allegedly.

I was drunk!
I just saw the long hair and went for it.

My time of the month...
on the set of porn-horror flick,
The Necro Files.
with Director Ron Carlo
in the background.

I'm a thirsty boy.
Needs must, and when the beer runs out...

Diving for hidden treasure in Whistler...

...without spilling a drop.

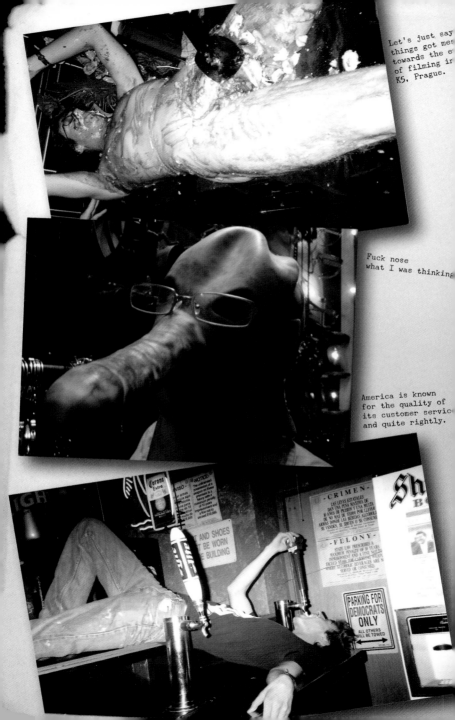

Let's just say
things got mes
towards the e
of filming in
K5, Prague.

Fuck nose
what I was thinking

America is known
for the quality of
its customer servic
and quite rightly.

dedicated to the art of the blowjob – with due scepticism. It was abundantly clear from the plush surroundings that the business was coining it in. The site showed one thing and one thing only: girls giving head, with the recipient recording the process on a hand-held camera in order to give the bloke's eye view of the action. I took a look at a couple of sample episodes and it was obvious why the site was such a hit. There was nothing complicated about it: the girls would walk into the room, strip off, get down on their knees and suck away, keeping their eyes squarely focused down the lens of the camera looking down at them. Any man will tell you that a girl looking up at you with your cock in her mouth is an incredibly erotic sight. These films captured those moments, and each of them invariably ended with a facial cum shot. It was utter filth... and utterly enchanting.

I sat down with John to have a chat about how we could cover this as a *Sin Cities* report. He suggested that I could film my own blowjob audition, explaining that there were already three girls in the building who would be taking part in a gang bang film later on that day. If I wanted, we could ask and see if we could use them to take part in our own film. This left me facing something of a dilemma. Was I comfortable with filming images – to be broadcast internationally and with no personal control over the edit – of my own sexual gratification? Not really... it sounded like a different film shoot altogether. Did I fancy getting sucked off by three-up-and-coming young porn stars? Yes. Decision made.

I am being slightly flippant there. In reality, I did have a bit of a moral struggle with this. If I was going to get sucked off by several girls who I had never met before on camera, I felt that somehow I was in danger of crossing an invisible line. If I was suddenly to appear on film getting blown by three budding porn stars, did that make me a porn actor? And importantly, would I end up looking like a complete twat?

What's difficult to explain here, in print, is what actually goes on behind the scenes, things that help to normalise the situation, to make it seem... more alright. It's not like you just show up, get some chicks together, throw them some cash and then demand that they get down on their hands and knees and suck dick. Don't get me wrong – I'm sure there are plenty of knob-ends working in porn who operate in such a brutal manner. For us though – and I'm not just saying this to justify my own connection to the industry – it was always a friendly, informal process. If there was ever any hint at 'funny business' then trust me, I would have jumped ship a long time ago.

In this instance, what happened is a bizarre conversation that took place between me and the girls who'd been earmarked to take part in my film. I went upstairs to meet them, all of them damn-fine-looking ladies, sitting upstairs on a sofa enjoying a pre-porno cigarette and cup of coffee. I joined them, explaining who I was and what we were planning.

I turned to the first girl and somewhat sheepishly asked her if she would be alright with sucking me off.

'Of course,' she replied.

'How about you, are you comfortable with that as well?' I asked, turning to the next girl.

'No problem,' she smiled.

'And you,' I asked the last girl, 'are you cool with this?'

'Sure, sounds like fun.'

Oh man, if only real life was like that. However, porn world is exactly that, and if you pardon the pun, there's no beating around the bush. As I stayed chatting with the girls, any moral dilemmas I'd had to begin with quickly disappeared. To me, however naïve or misplaced it may appear to the outsider, these girls appeared perfectly happy to take part in our film. Either that or they were brilliant actresses... and I suspected they were not. When I was satisfied that the girls were onside and that my film was a goer, I went back downstairs to psyche myself up for my big moment. Bearing in mind I was notorious for being unable to actually reach climax from oral sex, the girls would each have ten minutes in which to try and make me come. I wished the girls good luck, grabbed my camera and waited for contestant number one. Really, I'm not just making this up.

The first girl, Cassandra, was a petite Latina girl whose enthusiasm for sucking cock I had never before witnessed, have never since witnessed and very much doubt I will ever witness again. She grabbed my little fella, got it hard within seconds and then proceeded to give it an amazing session of undiluted joy. This girl guzzled like crazy. I was in ecstasy. Holding the camera pointing down at her, she looked up at me with her big brown eyes wide open, her mouth full and her breasts bouncing gently as she sucked back and forth. Wow. God, I love girls. Thinking back to that moment is actually making me deeply nostalgic, it was that good.

Despite the complete brilliance of Cassandra's technique, I was aware that there were two others waiting in the wings. It would be a crying shame if I didn't give them their opportunity to shine. I just about managed to hold myself together for the requisite ten minutes, helped at one point by seeing Denise's grinning face appearing around the corner to check up on my progress. Talk about putting you off your game. I politely told her to go swivel, and with the first ten minutes coming to a climax (or not, as the case was), a knock on the door signalled that the second girl would carry on seamlessly from where her companion had just left off. Oh dear Lord above, thank you, thank you.

And so another ten minutes passed and I was still on the receiving end of a top-class blowjob. True to form, though, I had yet to shoot my load and was eager to see if contestant number three could better the efforts of the previous girls. As number two sauntered off to attend to her newly acquired jaw-ache, the third girl took her position and went hell for leather for the honour of having me splurge in her face. She took to grabbing my boner, sucking it vigorously and then hitting herself in the face with it – a pleasant divergence from the earlier, more traditional techniques of the two preceding sessions. However, despite the brilliance of all three girls, I made it through to the half-hour point without the obligatory money-shot.

So what next? Well, how about a triple-header? Now there's a good idea. Within moments, I had all three girls kneeling down before me, one of them stuffing my cock in her mouth, another fondling my balls and the other licking my shaft. I can't easily describe the sexual buzz of this moment, let's just say it was truly monumental, a fantasy come true, a genuine thrill of gargantuan proportions – yep, that just about does it. All three girls gave it everything they had. However, despite the concentrated efforts of my new best friends, I had still failed to provide a triple facial. I think that holding the camera, and because several other people were now in the room bearing witness to my on-screen porn debut, I was distracted from the job in hand/mouth. Sensing the girls were approaching blowjob fatigue, and not wishing to inflict lockjaw on any of them, I decided to call a halt to proceedings. Besides, I had filmed nearly 40 minutes and was running out of tape – it was time to call it a wrap.

I had broken my porno duck, making an on-camera appearance in my first ever adult movie, and to my surprise, it had been an entirely guilt-free experience. Unfortunately it had also been, bizarrely for a porno, an orgasm-free incident. That said, my disappointment was tempered by the knowledge that my wank-bank would now have a new entry at number one – and trust me, it's one I continue to use to this day.

I did have a few concerns that I hadn't used a condom during this latest misdemeanour. I assumed that, as was usually standard in the porn industry, all the girls had had to provide proof that they were disease-free, but I wasn't entirely sure that that had been the case in this instance. And the more I thought about it, the more the risks were all too apparent. I mean, they weren't your average girls that you meet down The Falcon on a Friday night. They were regular hard-core porn performers, and judging by their blowjob skills, it was likely that mine was one of at least ten or twenty cocks that had been between their lips that very week. The last thing I needed on the road was a nasty dose of something nasty.

Back at the hotel and with paranoia starting to set in, I went for a quick chat with Denise and asked her if I should be worried about catching anything. As someone who had once been a bona fide groupie and had shagged, amongst many others, no less than two members of Guns N' Roses, Denise was, I considered, more qualified than most to know about the risks I had been running. She soon put my mind at rest by tossing me a small wrap of cocaine, a cunning way of distracting me from any negative thoughts about the health and safety of my knob. Wisely, I think, she told me to forget about it and to go out and enjoy a night off work – don't stay out too long, though, she warned, as early the next morning we were flying off to Vancouver.

Well, needless to say, ten hours later she was picking up the pieces once again as John and I staggered back

133

into the hotel lobby. We were absolutely munted. Predictably enough, we'd ended up going out for a complete monster of an evening in the heart of Montreal's seedier side of town and a heady mix of ketamine, cocaine and lager took a severe toll on us. Worse, our timing had been spectacularly bad – in less than two hours we were due to fly.

We hauled our kit into the waiting cab and after casually putting my hand in my pocket I discovered I still had several hundred dollars' worth of gear which I had bought towards the end of the night. Result! Going through customs with Class As would not be a good idea... not just because of the smuggling aspect, but mainly because I didn't want some guy's rubber-gloved hand up my jacksie. My next idea wasn't such a good one either – namely, to finish off the gear in the back of the cab. It made sense at the time and the last thing on my mind was to just toss it out the window. As we headed off, I lifted the wrap to my nose and snorted.

Denise looked on in disbelief. 'What the fuck are doing?!'

'I've got loads of this shit left. We'd better finish it off. Here,' I said, passing her some dodgy yellowish powder, 'dig in.'

With weary resignation and despite her fears that I was starting to lose the plot, Denise waded into my rapidly diminishing supply. In no time at all, we were at the airport, through customs and in the air. And I was relieved. And wasted. But happy.

Vancouver was home to yet another quality blowjob session, and one which had a more, shall we say, satisfying outcome. We'd heard that Mask TV, a website that let ordinary members of the public fulfil their sexual fantasies by featuring as Internet porn stars, was based in a huge tower block right in the centre of town. It sounded like ideal *Sin Cities* fodder. The idea behind the site was that people would log on and submit their ideas for a fantasy sex scene and then the web site would set it up for them. In return, it would be filmed and posted on Mask TV's site. The participants retained anonymity by wearing an assortment of masks, hence the name.

I put a lot of thought into what my own particular fantasy would be and having spent, hmmm, literally seconds putting together a script, I had come up with the not entirely original concept of playing the role of a big-shot company boss who would interview a secretary for a new job. Whether her application was successful or not would depend on her enthusiasm for granting me sexual favours. Perfick.

I was introduced to my co-star, Amy, a girl of Chinese origin who confessed to being crap at acting but was nevertheless a budding porn starlet. Go figure. Luckily, we weren't interested in producing high art. I sat down with Amy and went through some possible scenarios for the shoot. My main concern at that point was not for her to learn her lines (there wasn't a lot of talking in the script) but to work out some parameters of what she was comfortable doing and where her sexual limits lay. Oddly, I still didn't really know where my own limits were and how far I was actually prepared to go. I decided I'd take the lead from my fellow thespian. She told me she was a specialist in choking videos but was 'happy to do anything apart from full-on sex.'

Well, that suited me fine. And as far as her expertise in choking was concerned, well, I was happy to leave that well alone for the moment. Regardless of how mental it seems, the way I got my head round it was to think it wasn't so different from having sex with someone I'd just met at a bar and gone on to have a one-night stand with.

I mean, how much meaningful conversation do you actually have with someone before you end up shagging? In my experience, sometimes very little. That said, I think if I hadn't clicked with Amy, I would have done things differently. But fuck it. I was single, felt perfectly at ease with her and was more than happy to get the show on the road.

Having set up a studio as a makeshift office, I took my seat behind a desk sporting a flash suit and the obligatory red braces. I began puffing away on a huge cigar as I waited for a knock on the door from the eager applicant. Knowing you're only minutes away from a top-notch porn star blowjob is, trust me, a good place to be. I composed myself and got into character, somewhere between Donald Trump and well, me, I suppose. As the cameras rolled, Amy and I moved from a brief chat, into some fondling, and then, joy of joys, my potential secretary sunk to her knees and went in for the gobble. I was struggling to keep a straight face as I considered my next line.

'Right, let's discuss your contract shall we?' (Slurp, slurp...) 'How does fifteen bucks a week sound?' I asked, and then immediately burst out laughing. A succession of giggling fits and endless takes later, and, lucky me, some cracking blowjob action, and we finally had our movie in the bag. As the director put down the camera, Amy continued gobbing me off and then looked up at me.

'Hey Ashley, aren't you going to come?'

'Er... well, we've finished filming. We're done.'

'So what?' she replied, still munching away. 'Don't let that worry you, I want you to come, I love it... please... come in my mouth.'

To hear someone pleading for you to cum is an invitation that few men in their right mind will ever turn down, and I was no exception. I looked over to my director.

'Hey John, can I just stay in here for a while? And if you could close the door on your way out please... cheers mate.'

Game on. With no film crew to distract me and a girl who was eager for some nutrient-heavy face paint I duly proceeded to change the habit of a lifetime. And blowjobs had officially become my new favourite thing.

chapter 13
cocaine and prostitutes

With moments like we had in Canada scattered throughout the filming process, I was very happy working in television. Despite the fact that such pleasurable moments were sometimes overshadowed by the pain and sometimes plain boredom of the milder S&M scene, on the whole I loved being on the *Sin Cities* road. I adored staying in hotels, seeing new places, and sampling the nightspots of different cities and cultures. My lifestyle back in England had always been fairly debauched, and that trend continued. But as I'd already found out, living it up could also have its downsides. I had already been tipped over the edge after my *Bad Trip* experience. And then during *Sin Cities*, a visit to Argentina took me close to paying the full price.

We arrived in the capital, Buenos Aires, full of optimism – I'd always wanted to visit South America and it didn't disappoint. I was instantly struck by the beauty of the girls in Argentina – even walking down the street, I felt like a kid in a candy store. From a random selection of ten girls, I would have classed at least five of them as gorgeous and another three as genuinely stunning. The other two weren't bad either. Filming non-stop since our arrival had meant there wasn't any time to go out and try our luck, but once the show was in the bag, we found ourselves with a couple of days free before we were due to head back to Europe. A big night out was in order.

Amidst a flurry of booze, I ended up winning a bet with my then camera-man, Rob Bloomfield, in which the winner would be to be treated to a paid-up visit from a prostitute. After a few more hours on the town, however, I innocently assumed that my winning prize had been forgotten – but what the hell, that suited me fine. By then I was far too drunk to contemplate sex. I made it back to my hotel room and collapsed into bed to get some shut-eye. Before I fell into a drunken coma, there was a knock on the door. I was certain I hadn't ordered room service. Once I'd wrestled the door open, there she was.

'Hi. Your friend invited me up to see you. He said you wanted to have some fun tonight.'

Helped by the fact that Rob had now poked his head around the side of the door, grinning inanely, I suddenly remembered the wager. Gulp. Here we go.

'Wow. Hello. What's your name?'

I forget the name, but let's call her Blondie. Blondie walked brazenly into my room and sat down at the table.

'You want some coke?'

I was thinking of plenty of reasons why doing some lines with a prostitute I'd only just met was an exceptionally bad idea, but instead I heard myself agreeing. There are times when even if I know things are a bad idea, I still do them just to see what happens. This was one of those times... I was about to hit the self-destruct button.

Blondie was a great-looking girl; sexy, slender and

petite but with a cracking cleavage. She was lively, up front and seemed perfectly at home in a matter of minutes. Rob and I looked on as she pulled out a small bag of party powder and racked up three fat lines. One rolled-up note, a sharp sniff and I was shifted sideways from feeling a bit drunk and woozy to feeling high and horny. Rob looked at me and decided his arse could be in danger. Secretly, I was hoping he'd scarper – I was up for a threesome but preferably with two girls. Luckily for me, he'd had enough and saluted me goodbye. The door closed, Blondie flicked back her hair, looked at me and smiled.

'Come on, let's go to bed,' she said.

What else could I do? I didn't want to waste Rob's money. Blondie and I immediately clicked in the bedroom. As you probably well know, cocaine is a drug that cranks up your sex drive and, Christ, by now it had taken full effect. The other thing it does – for me in any case – is prolong staying power, and in this instance, it looked like I was on course for a sexual marathon.

We hit the sack and before long Blondie was crying out for me to cum – but that was a long way off yet. One quick session and I was out of breath and needing a quick break.

'We do another line, yes?'

'Yes. Of course we do another line. Several.'

I joined her back at the table where a full gram had been emptied to form four enormous lines – looked like we were going shotgun. I fired one up each nostril and the rush of chemicals hit me like a hammer. I was blitzed. I stood up and sucked down a swig of beer. More sex please, I'm Superman.

We jumped back into bed. I was totally in the moment, rampant, wanting to devour her, and she was crying out for me to cum and I wanted that feeling of release. God, how I wanted it. I concentrated and focused on her breasts crashing back and forth to the motion of my body, hoping it would get me there. It was no use though, I'm usually done and dusted after about ten minutes (sad, I know) and we'd been going for well over half an hour and I was spent. My heart was racing and I needed to give it a break.

'You don't like me? Why don't you cum?'

'No,' I quickly reply. 'I think you're great. I just need to rest a second.'

It turned out that I wasn't Superman, and Blondie was in no mood for rest. She reached over and took out another wrap of coke but this time she didn't bother to cut a line out. Instead she opened it up, lifted it to her nose and took one almighty snort. Ouch. Was this is reaching new heights... or lows? I was starting to feel ever so slightly concerned about being out of my depth. I didn't know this girl, she'd been in my room for about an hour, and I was completely mullered. And she also started to look pretty wired; eyes wild, swallowing a lot. When she looked at her watch I felt relieved... maybe my time was up and she'd soon be gone. No such luck.

'Shall I go and get some more coke?' she asked. 'I've run out.'

I just thought she was saying that as an excuse to leave. I mean, as soon as she left, she wasn't likely to return was she? I gave her a bit of money to contribute to the coke fund, but I was really giving it to her as a tip for visiting me and sharing her gear. With that, Blondie dressed, kissed me goodbye and left the room. There's no chance of sleep after that much coke. My eyes were fixed open and I knew I was looking at the distinct possibility of not sleeping until the following night. At least.

And then, half an hour later... a knock on the door. Are you fucking kidding me? Nope. Sure enough, Blondie strolled back in, threw me a cursory 'hello' and dropped four new wraps of coke down on the table. This night... day... whatever it was... was never going to end. It was around six o'clock in the morning and starting to look like plenty more less-than-quality-time was ahead of us. I wasn't entirely happy about the situation. The coke will soon sort that out, Ash: here, take this. I took the note and snorted up another huge dose of gack. By this point, I was fully aware that it was a lot purer than the stuff I'm used to back at home. As well as making me instantly high, the comedown was quicker, leaving me wanting another dose in a far shorter space of time. In short, it was very more-ish.

'Hey,' she says, 'how about we go over to my flat?'

Why on earth would I want to do that – with someone I only know in my coke-riddled mind as Blondie? I didn't think it was a particularly bright idea at all, but my friend Charlie did. And before I knew it, I was walking up some stairs holding Blondie's hand, about to go into her apartment.

'Nice place,' I say. And it is.

Blondie is obviously doing pretty well in her chosen line of business; she has a sleek, modern one-bed flat. Her mobile phone keeps ringing and she puts on a seductive whore's voice to answer it. On the other end of the line will be another client. What am I doing with this girl? More coke, that's what. By now, I'm chomping at the bit and want to get stuck into some more drugs.

A couple more lines each. Another quick romp in bed. Then I need a top-up. Find the coke. A fresh wrap. Empty it on the glass surface and feel greedy. Do the lot... one gram in one line, I've never done that before. I crouch down, hover over it, then just snort the whole thing up my sneck in one go. Holy shit! I stand up, I'm swaying. Whoa, Ash. Slow down! But it's way too late for that.

142

Jesus. I'm starting to sweat. This is seriously strong stuff.

The phone rings again and Blondie's sex voice kicks into action. Then I'm not so sure I feel so good anymore. Yeah, you're worried now, aren't you? Better lie down on the bed, that'll sort you out. Lie down on the bed. Where's the bed? The bed's over there. Better lie down on the bed. Lie down. Bed. I'm on the bed. My heart. What's happening to my heart? Oh my God, it's pumping like fuck! I can hear it banging against my rib cage. Each heartbeat is merging into one as it speeds along like an express train. Then I hear the flush of the toilet. Blondie's coming back. Bang-bang-bang. I look up at the ceiling. It won't keep still. I don't feel right. I'm at the polar fucking opposite of feeling right. Then Blondie comes into focus and she's looking down at me.

'Are you OK?'

'I don't think so. I don't feel so good.'

An understatement, if ever there was one. I was really, really fucked up. Blondie had a bad look in her eyes – the look of fear, alarm and outright panic. I knew what that look meant. It meant that this English boy, who she didn't know, looked like he may be on the verge of an overdose and would probably die right there on her bed. And that's what I was starting to think too. Fucking hell Ashley, you idiot! My heart was still pumping like a bastard (still a good sign at that point) and the cocaine smashing its way round my system. Death was becoming a real possibility.

'Shall I call someone?' she asked.

'No. No, don't do that.'

Shit, if Blondie was thinking in terms of ambulance and emergency services, then I really was in a bad place. And I think, looking back, that this was the only time in my life where I have ever seriously thought I was in genuine danger of keeling over and dying. How was I going to get out of this one? Dig deep. Deal with it. Dig really, really deep. And then at that moment all I could think about was my parents. My parents, who had nurtured me and look after me, sacrificed so much to pay for my education, encouraged and loved me every step of the way, and this, *this* was how I was going to repay them – by dying of a drugs overdose on the bed of a hooker in South America? This, I think, was one of those times when you have to take stock of your life, look deep inside yourself and try and do something, *anything*, to make things better. Unless I moved from that bed, I was certain I'd die on it. Do that Ashley, do that! Get off the fucking bed! Show some signs of life!

From somewhere, I don't know where, I found some residue of inner strength and lifted myself off the bed. Do something to slow that heart beat down. Breathe slowly. In, out, in, out. And again, slower this time. That's better, try to relax. Think good thoughts, drink some water. Keep breathing; always remember to breathe.

Blondie helped me over to the sink and I started taking in mouthfuls of water. That's better. Oh, beautiful! That is *so* much better. My heart beat slowed and stopped thumping so hard. Such a fucking relief. Thank you, Blondie, thank you. Next thing, get some fresh air. I need to leave, be on my own, walk around a bit, pull myself together. There. I was going to be OK.

'Hey, it's been a blast. [You can fucking say that again, you monkey]. But I'd better leave now,' I said.

Blondie looked at me and nodded. She'd be glad to see the back of me. We hugged our goodbyes. It had been some adventure, I suspect not just for me, but for the both of us. I needed to get back to my hotel, settle down, get healthy and calm down a bit. Yet again, an almost suicidal urge to get my kicks had turned into what I am convinced had been a very close call. Thank God it was all over; I wouldn't be doing that again in a hurry. Well, not for a couple of weeks at least. As I was leaving, Blondie's phone rang again. This time, she didn't answer.

Sex with a prostitute is a difficult thing to talk about and I'm really wary of writing about it because I obviously don't want you to think I'm a complete wanker. By saying, 'Yep, I've had sex with hookers,' I'm aware that I'm in danger of tumbling into that category. But is it really so bad? In principle, is anything wrong with a consenting man or a woman choosing to pay for sexual contact or to charge for it? I think like a lot of other controversial subjects, a lot of society's negativity is down to prejudice and lack of knowledge. Just as I have met and hung out with porn stars, so have I met and shared time with prostitutes. Believe it or not, they're just like you and me: some are happy in their job and some are not. Difference is, their job happens to be far more… niche.

I don't want to be frivolous about this because I know I still harbour a very real sense of guilt, shame and sadness after paying for sex, so I've obviously got some issues with it myself. Not least, I'm connecting myself with what many perceive to be a world of abuse and exploitation. I'm not entirely certain if I'm sufficiently intellectually equipped to express exactly how I feel about that. I feel flawed is probably the best way of putting it. Another way is by saying that I feel like a fucking loser by resorting to prostitutes. But that's not always the case. Sometimes it can be fun and be a transaction entirely sans guilt – and those times are invariably when you get a sense that the girl is really enjoying her work. Now, I'm sure some of the more cynical among you will doubtless be thinking that a prostitute that enjoys having sex with paying customers is just a myth, a male invention. But you'd be wrong. Sometimes – shock horror – hookers do actually enjoy themselves. But as I'm writing this, I would concede that that's probably a rarity. I think most working girls are probably gritting their teeth during the vast majority of their encounters with a paying customer. I also think I'm probably wrapping myself up in self-denial here by saying it can be a guilt-free experience. When prostitution is so closely married to substance abuse, economic inequalities, violence, pimping and criminality, it's hard to look in the mirror afterwards and not feel a very acute sense of shame.

When talking about prostitution, it's no surprise that girls in particular seem to find it difficult to relate to a sexual experience where it's a purely physical act rather than an emotional one. Having said that, women use male prostitutes too, so I guess prostitution is catering for a need that is both male and female. On the whole though, it's nothing new to suggest that men find it far easier to indulge in carnal pleasures without considering any 'relationship' issues, and I'm no exception to that rule. I suppose where I am perhaps a bit different from most other men is that, while it may put me in the doghouse, I'm prepared to bite the bullet and openly admit to having paid for sex. Most men, in order to save face, a relationship, or their reputation, will deny it. However, depending on which research you believe, then prostitution is not just the oldest profession, it's also one of the most endemic. I remember reading a feature in a magazine a couple of years ago about the number of men who admitted using prostitutes, saying the figure had doubled between 1995 and 2000. Something like four percent admitted having paid for sex in the previous five years, and one in ten over a lifetime. So, around ten percent of men have apparently used the services of a professional. Another snippet I remember was about some research carried out in Sweden. There, the figure was around one in eight adult men have paid for sex at least once and the majority of them are or have been married or in a relationship. So, that tells us that it isn't just the archetypical man-in-a-raincoat who likes to indulge... it is grandfathers, fathers, husbands, sons and brothers. There were around 80,000 people employed in the sex trade in the UK at the time of the article, which as it was a couple of years ago, I assume has increased.

Does this sound like I'm using statistics to justify my own dubious moral standards? Hmm, I probably am. Worse, I'd say that nowadays I'm pretty much a seasoned pro – I try not to make it a habit, but I have to confess that I can, just like my indulgences with drink and drugs, sometimes embark on some kind of shagging binge. In terms of what I think about myself for using prostitutes, well, as you've probably gathered, I'm torn; there's conflict. The laddish part of me wants to stand up and say 'it's fucking exciting and great – hookers are ace fun' and that version of events would, occasionally, be true. But another other part of me would say that using prostitutes is a very soul-destroying experience. If I stand back and analyse it, then I'm also the product of my society where everything, including sex, is increasingly available and disposable. I don't deny that that's quite a sad and depressing conclusion.

But what about the prostitute? What does she think about the punter? And how does she cope mentally and physically with the demands of the job? Obviously I can't speak for the working girl herself, so for this part of the book I decided to get on the Internet, do a quick search and see if I could get someone to talk to me about this. I got lucky – believe it or not, the first lady I emailed, who went by the name of Mia, agreed to talk to me. I had chosen her completely randomly but it turned out she had seen *Sin Cities* and was well up for a chat with yours truly. She invited me round to her flat, charging me £200 for the pleasure but promising to throw in a few extras if I behaved myself. Bargain.

Mia met me at the door in a very revealing black corset, sat me down on the bed, and I fired off my first question.

Ashley: So Mia, what term should I use for what you do? Are you a prostitute, hooker, whore, working girl... how do I refer to you?
Mia: I like working girl.

Me: Why not prostitute? What's wrong with that?
Her: It's very old fashioned, I think.

Me: If someone who lived round here found out what you did and called you a whore to your face, how would you react to that?
Her: It depends. I see prostitution as a profession. So if I was to be offended it would only be about the context in which it was said.

Me: Tell me how you started off as a filthy whore then.
Her: [Laughs] Well, when I was younger I didn't have much money but I had a lot of ambition and wanted to better myself. My mum had a business which she was never successful at, my dad stopped work when I was six or seven years old and I saw them struggling and decided I didn't want to be like that. I was living in a third-world country and I was more or less a third class citizen and it doesn't get much lower than that. I was working in a club waitressing and met an English guy who invited me to the UK. I came over, the relationship didn't work out and I so I was left on my

own. I went to college for two years and qualified as a beauty therapist. I then found work in a beauty salon where I struggled and struggled and never really got anywhere, so I decided to sell myself, and that's why we're here now.

Me: So what happened next?
Her: I saw an advert in the newspaper, met a working girl and she introduced me to an agency and I decided to give it a go.

Me: What was it like when you got your first booking? Were you nervous?
Her: Yes, at that time I was always nervous.

Me: And you went on to have sex for money... what was that like for you?
Her: Exciting. A lot of adrenaline. A bit scared.

Me: Was it just normal, vanilla sex?
Her: It was, if you call oral sex normal. By today's standards, then yes. It was not 'normal' by my standards at the time.

Me: What do you mean by that?
Her: I wasn't used to giving oral. It took me quite a while to get into it. I'd had a lot of experience sexually but not in the way where you suck a man's cock or he licks you out – that's a cultural thing. Where I came from, you don't give blowjobs and you don't let the man go down on you, so I was lacking in experience in that department.

Me: Crikey. Sounds like my kind of place then – you just kiss someone and fuck them. Sod the foreplay!

Her: [Laughs] Yes!

Me: So when you were younger, apart from oral, did you always like sex and put it about a bit? How many sexual partners did you have, say, before you were 21?
Her: It would be a lot. I didn't count. Probably about forty.

Me: So you had your first client, what was it like afterwards when you went home? Do you think to yourself that you've crossed a line there and that I'm now selling my body? Did you have any moral issues with that?
Her: I did. But in an exciting way. It was taboo. I was like... 'Oh no, I've really gone and done it now!'

Me: That's interesting. I think the feeling you're expressing there, of what's taboo, is also what a lot of clients feel about seeing a working girl themselves. That's what they pay for. It's not just the sex, it's also getting ready for it and then having the thought of doing something naughty that you wouldn't tell your parents about – the feeling of rebelling. That's all part of the rush, I think.
Her: Yes. I still get that adrenaline rush meeting a client for the first time. The excitement of 'My God, we're gonna fuck!' There are all those questions in your head – is he going to be nice? What's his attitude going to be like? What will he look like?

Me: How do I figure on that front?
Her: Pretty cool [laughs].

Me: So your doorbell goes, your customer's there. He's old and fat and he's someone you wouldn't give a second glance to in the street, and yet you're going to have sex with him... or not?

Her: Well I don't just open the door – I can see from the camera who's outside. I then have a choice to make – a split-second decision. Am I in the mood for some? You know, because it's really taboo, you know, a dodgy old man... do I want to fuck him... do I feel like I'm in that mood, a slutty mood, and if I am, I go and I open the door and I'm happy to oblige. If I'm not I'll just switch the doorbell off and eventually he'll go away.

Me: Do you have any preferences in what you like physically in a guy?

Her: I have preferences in size. According to the mood I'm in I like something that's small, medium and large.

Me: We're talking cock here then?

Her: Yes.

Me: And you must have seen a lot of cock.

Her: I've seen my fair share.

Me: What's the biggest?

Her: About 12 and a half, 13 inches.

Me: Jesus! That's about twice my size!

Her: Oh, I see. Average. That's alright.

Me: Did you fuck the guy?

Her: Yes, but not in the arse.

Me: And how was that?

Her: Uncomfortable but exciting.

Me: And what about the smallest?
Her: Brilliant for arse-fucking.

Me: So all is not lost if you have a tiny penis?
Her: Absolutely not. I love a small cock in the arse.

Me: And what about medium then? The best of both worlds?
Her: Yes.

Me: So I'm good to go then?
Her: Yes.

Me: What do you think the guys who visit you are looking for?
Her: It's the excitement of having sex with someone they really desire.

Me: And when you're having sex with someone, what's going through your mind?
Her: I'm in the moment. I'm thinking of how he feels inside me. That's what I focus on when I'm working – I'm enjoying the moment.

Me: Is it always enjoyable though? Are you being honest?
Her: Yes. I love it. It's natural. Each to their own, but that's my perspective. Sure, sometimes there are outside factors that affect how I feel in the bedroom but that's not the client's fault. Sometimes it can take me time to get into it but usually I really enjoy it.
Me: Are there any clients who you dread to see returning?
Her: There's one particular client who loves to book overnight with me but the problem is that his cock is

so big and thick and he loves arse-fucking. He just fucks and fucks and fucks the whole night. I don't get a break so sometimes I try to intoxicate him with alcohol so that he falls asleep. He arrives at around 9pm and leaves at 7am and in that time he fucks at least five times. He doesn't necessarily always cum but it's just fuck fuck fuck for like an hour each time. For him, when he calls, sometimes I'll say I'm busy when it's not necessarily true.

Me: Let's talk numbers. How many punters do you think you see in the average week?
Her: Hmmm, I'd say I usually get into double figures most weeks.

Me: And do they all want sex?
Her: It varies. Some weeks all of them will fuck me and other weeks, maybe only half.

Me: So we're talking around five or six hundred sex partners a year... that's a lot, Mia. How do you feel about that in your head?
Her: Pretty darn good.

Me: You don't have darker moments when you think 'Christ, what am I doing?'
Her: No. I don't. I don't have any psychological hang-ups about it. I tell you honestly, what gets me down is when it's a slow week, when I'm not as busy as normal.

Me: You must have done some pretty odd things. What's the weirdest thing someone has asked you to do for money?
Her: I had a client here about three days ago and he

wanted to know if I had any used condoms in the bin. He wanted to drink the sperm from them and for me to watch him do that. He wanted to empty them in his mouth in front of me – to drink all the sperm and for me to beat him up as punishment if he didn't finish the lot. But I wasn't in the mood for it, so I told him there weren't any.

Me: Did that shock you when he asked to do that?
Her: Well, I thought I'd heard it all before, but this was a new one!

Me: Give me another example of the more outlandish requests you've had.
Her: Well, I've crapped in someone's mouth and had them eat it. I get a sense of power from that. I feel in control, I feel very dominant. It's taboo and exciting, but there's also part of you that just gets on with the job and you just do it. You know, it's something that the client enjoys and he pays good money for it, so 'give him the shit' is what I say.

Me: Does it not seem extraordinary to you that some-one would pay another person to lay a turd in their mouth?
Her: Well this person is a regular of mine. He owns a chain of restaurants.

Me: Does he actually eat the poo?
Her: Yes. He swallows it.

Me: Does he brush his teeth afterwards?
Her: No. He cleans the outside of his mouth but likes to leave with the smell.

Me: Do you know if he's married?

Her: He is. When his wife goes away he likes to get really nasty.

Me: Do you feel in some way complicit in some kind of betrayal of her?

Her: I don't have that moral issue. If I did, the job would be pretty hard because of the amount of people I fuck on a regular basis. If I felt guilty I would end up needing therapy, so I clearly don't have that type of feeling. It's just a service that I provide, an exchange.

Me: Does it ever go beyond that? Do you ever get emotionally attached to some of your clients?

Her: I've met clients that I really like so in that sense, yes. But it's just phases that I seem to go through. I assume it's the same for them because sometimes I'll see them on a very regular basis, then it just tapers off when they've probably found someone else. But within that period of time there is that connection.

Me: So do you ever feel that you're not just having sex, you're having a relationship?

Her: With some clients, in an abstract kind of way, yes.

Me: Have you ever fallen in love with any customers?

Her: Not yet. But there are some who I have really, really liked.

Me: Are there any sexual fantasies that you've had and which you've successfully enacted with a client?

Her: Yes, I always wanted to fuck someone up the arse though I am yet to watch any of my clients sucking another man's cock and then be fucked by it – that has

155

always been one of my big fantasies. In fact, that's well up there at the top of my to-do list.

Me: What about girl-on-girl stuff: do you ever get women asking for services?
Her: Sometimes, yes. Some are bisexuals who bring their partners. I'm not bi-sexual so I'll kiss the girl and play with her breasts and finger her pussy. But I won't eat pussy – I've tried it but it's just not for me. Then I might have sex with her partner while she watches or I'll watch them having sex.

Me: Who's your most unusual client?
Her: One that stands out in my head is a guy who couldn't possibly be any younger than 95 years old. He's a lovely man. He's got a nice, average cock. And even though he's between 95 and 100 years old, he always gets nice and hard. And it's a great feeling for me that I can help someone like that. And he's just old, you know, I like to think that I don't discriminate against older men.

Me: So what's going to happen in the future? Do you feel a sense of impending doom that nature will take its course; you'll reach fifty and no longer be so desirable?
Her: Well, I've just bought a four-bedroom house abroad and I'm now studying for a law degree, so hopefully by the time I'm fifty I'll be laughing and thinking about the thousands of men I've licked, sucked and fucked and who paid for it all. I'm very grateful, thank you.

I guess Mia could have added 'shat on' to that list. And whoever that guy is who ate and digested her shit: mate,

I hope you get well soon... next time, do us all a favour and brush your teeth afterwards. As for Mr-I-Want-To-Drink-Semen-From-Condoms... for once, I'm truly lost for words.

As far as the actual nuts and bolts that lie behind the process leading up to an encounter with a sex worker, well, I found Mia by plugging into the Internet – something which has made things a lot different from a decade ago. No longer do you have to scour the Yellow Pages for the Escort section or traipse the streets and phone a calling card from a telephone box in town. Instead, an Internet search will take you, within a matter of seconds, headlong into a virtual sex emporium and hundreds of readily available girls.

There are usually three main options – you can go to a massage parlour or brothel with a selection of several girls, or you can call up an escort agency (of which there are hundreds in the UK) and ask to see one of the girls on their books. Alternatively, you can call direct and book an appointment with a girl who works independently – she will either visit you, or the slightly cheaper option (usually by £50) is to go round to her place. Seeing an independent working girl would always be my preference. If you take any other option there's a far greater possibility that you're entering the more morally dubious arena of human trafficking and girls coerced into selling themselves.

The first thing a newcomer to the scene would probably notice is how an entire language of abbreviations has evolved around the industry. I've looked into it for you, so no need to worry. The jargon used to describe what services a particular girl offers usually includes the following:

COF	cum on face
CIM	cum in mouth
COB	cum on body
GS	golden shower (pissing)
WS	water-sports (as above)
OWO	oral without (no condom)
BBBJ	bare-back blow job (as above)
PSE	porn star experience
GFE	girlfriend experience
DFK	deep French kissing

Why anyone would want DFK with someone who may, for all the client knows, have just finished doing OWO and CIM with another customer just minutes before is utterly beyond me, but there you go.

In terms of price you'll pay anything from around £150 to £350 for all of those services, including MSOG (multiple shots on goal) in a single hour-long session. Seriously. An overnight stay with the girl of your choice will set you back about a grand. Again though, for me, the idea of paying for more than an hour with someone seems pointless. In fact, that's exactly the kind of encounter I'm trying to avoid when I pay for a prostitute: if I wanted a one-night stand with someone, then I'd go out and find it – why pay? I'm paying not really so much for the sex, rather the fact that I can just have straight-up sex and not have to bother attempting to form any meaningful relationship. In my case, then, the famed Jack Nicholson quote 'You don't pay them to fuck you, you pay them to leave,' does ring true. You're also paying for minimal conversation, no arguments, no emotional heartache and sometimes, yes, you're paying for a truly monumental shag.

Usually though, I find it's a complete waste of money. I'm not the most sensitive soul in the world, but still, for me, any physical pleasure is invariably offset by far too much self-analysis, guilt, shame and, in the end, regret. So why go back and pay for sex a second, third, or even a fourth time? Well, I'm an eternal optimist. Usually it's pretty obvious as soon as you meet your chosen lady whether it'll be a rare triumph or the usual disaster – like in a normal encounter at a bar or a nightclub, it's all about chemistry.

The first time I ever paid for sex I was in my early twenties and had just moved to London. It was, I imagine, a fairly typical experience: I was very, very drunk, staggering around Leicester Square late at night and saw one of those small, hand-written signs against a non-descript open door – 'Girl Upstairs'. I staggered in, went up some tattered old stairs and into an open living room in which were sat a middle-aged woman and a younger blonde girl who was about the same age as me. I muttered briefly about seeing the sign downstairs, handed over 40-odd quid and was then taken through to the bedroom by the blonde girl. And that was my initiation into the sex trade. I think what made the biggest impact for me was how swiftly you could go from seeing a sign to suddenly having penetrative sex – probably about three or four minutes in my case.

I remember while in the act of sex looking down at the girl beneath me: a semi-attractive but utterly disinterested girl. Fulfilling sex it was not... seedy, sordid and lowlife, it most definitely was. I remember feeling pretty bad about the whole squalid transaction. Prostitutes, as we all know, are human beings with feelings too, and as I quite like human beings, I obviously wanted her to enjoy the experience. But this girl quite plainly wanted to see the back of me as soon as humanly possible. Heck, she didn't even attempt to muster up any simulated sense of enjoyment. Fair enough – I wouldn't have bothered either.

And then it got even worse.

'Can we change position please?' I asked, desperate to do something to change the vibe.

'Christ,' she replied. 'Can't you hurry up?'

Gee, that's a bit harsh. I know you can get the full girlfriend experience, but that sounded too close to the real thing. After rolling her eyes towards the ceiling, she turned round and got on all fours. In my battered state I floundered aimlessly on my knees behind her. Then she started getting impatient, sighing and turning to glare at me. Fucking hell! It was about as far from the Belle De Jour fantasy fuck as you could possibly go. Who could blame her though? There I was, some young twat in off the street... just another dickhead customer, and absolutely arse-holed. She grabbed my cock and shoved it back inside her and we started back up again, but I simply couldn't be bothered to carry on. I was too drunk. The whole sorry scene had turned me off something rotten and I wanted to leave this girl alone rather than inflict any more obligations upon her. As quickly as possible, I gathered up my clothes, swallowed down an extra-large helping of self-hatred, and left. 'Fuck that. I won't ever be doing that again,' I thought to myself. But of course, I did – which is even more surprising when you bear in mind that my second encounter was equally, if not more fucked up.

I remember taking off from England one day shortly after leaving university and somehow or other, a few weeks later, I ended up in Prague. I had been there for over a week living in some shoddy student accommodation and keeping myself to myself. Bored and slightly restless one night, I headed off into town. As I walked around the main streets, some scantily-clad working girls whistled at me as I walked past.

160

'Psssssst! Hey, you looking for something, honey?'

I ignored them and went off to a bar to get tanked up on some cheap local booze. It was almost morning as I started to make my way home, and by that time I was pretty loaded and headed back towards the main square. The streets were deserted at that point – all the groups of prostitutes I saw earlier were nowhere to be seen until I headed down towards the subway. I was approached by a girl who, with my beer goggles on, looked to me like an absolute fucking stunner. I looked at her, slowed my step and she moved towards me... we both knew what we wanted. Her – money, me – a fuck. And she really was gorgeous, with long dark hair and a body to die for, all perfectly packaged in a revealing red dress. I don't remember exactly how things progressed; I think she stopped and asked me the time and then I asked her if she wanted to come back home with me.

'Sure, if you have money,' came the reply. When I asked her how much it cost, she explained that she would take me to a hotel and I would have to pay for her and for the room. I started to scrabble around for money in my pockets.

'No, not here, not here! The police! Be careful.'

She was right. I was hardly very subtle about it, but neither were her red dress and stilettos. Various bits of crap spilled from my pockets onto the street. I pulled myself together and we headed towards a nearby hotel. As I counted out some money, the girl started speaking to the receptionist to book a room. It was then that the level-headed middle-class voice in my head piped up: 'Jesus, Ash, what the fuck are you getting yourself into?'

A combination of drunkenness and an impulsive desire for action chose to ignore the question. Meanwhile, agreement on the room was reached and the girl told me it would cost such-and-such an amount, and then I

161

realised I had nowhere near enough cash. As the girl and I walked off together, I started to apologise, explaining that I didn't have enough money on me. The Czech girl looked at me as though I was an idiot (I was). Then, instead of doing the sensible thing and telling me to fuck off, she told me to follow her.

'Do you have bank card? We try to get money out,' she said. She was full of good ideas, and they all involved me handing over money.

So we headed off to find a cash machine and like in so many other drunken moments, I was torn between wanting to do the sensible thing (say goodbye, go home, get some kip), and wanting to revel in the excitement of finding myself on the brink of a new and possibly thrilling adventure. The balance began to shift considerably towards wanting to go home as we approached a group of somewhat tarty looking girls and a couple of large, scary looking, shaven-headed Eastern European men. Some words of Czech passed between them and a few cursory glances were thrown in my direction.

'Fuck it,' I thought. 'Why don't I just sod off home?'

But it was too late for that. My new lady friend took me by the arm and spoke in broken English: 'No cash machine here. How much money you have?'

I show her. There's probably about £20 kicking around in loose change and a couple of battered old notes.

'Give to me, come with me... is not enough but I give you hand-job.'

Jeepers creepers. So anyway, we rounded the corner and she stopped me by the side of some non-descript building. Then (someone please shoot me) she put her hand down my trousers and started wanking me off. Jesus Christ! So all those valuable years at school and university had led me down a path to this?! I mean, fucking hell. It was insane: there I was in the centre of town, stood on the street, with a hooker, admittedly a stunning one but a hooker nonetheless, with her hand in my pants, my cock protruding from out of my jeans... and daylight was breaking. Oh God! It was so fucking wrong! A couple of minutes passed and all that was going through my mind was that I could end up getting arrested. What the hell was I thinking?

Sometimes I really do wonder what the fuck is going on in my head to make me think that stuff like this could possibly pass as rational behaviour. I mean obviously something is not quite right in my head... is it just that I'm drunk... or is it something more sinister than that? Or is it just youthful exuberance? I wasn't asking myself any of these questions at the time, I was really just intent on getting the fuck out of Dodge, which after seeing a couple of early morning shift workers in the distance, I eventually did.

'I'm sorry, I have to go. I really must go home.' I blurted out. 'Sorry and thank you.'

And with that, I staggered off into the distance. Put that one down to experience, Ashley, and don't ever do that again, you fucking numb-nut.

So, if I think back to these disastrous occasions, why would I ever return to have sex with a prostitute? It's happened since and, in spite of everything, I don't rule out the possibility that it will happen again. This may sound odd, but I would compare it to drugs – the first time I ever did coke, for instance, I wondered what all the hoo ha was about. It was no great shakes. But then after a few more goes, you start to get to grips with how to use and become more comfortable and excited by it. And then later on, too much familiarity starts to breed boredom, contempt and self-hatred. What then becomes attractive is not the actual act of taking drugs (or the actual act of having sex) but the journey to that point – buying the coke, going to the pub, sneaking a visit to the toilet, unwrapping a gram, cutting out a line... and then, well, the snort and the hit are just the start of a long comedown. It's the same with sex and prostitution – in the moments after having made the call to see a working girl; I'm already starting to get a buzz off the thought that I'm now only an hour or so away from sex with someone I've never even met. The sex itself is almost an irrelevance.

It is a weird feeling, an exciting feeling as you're walking down the street contemplating what lies ahead... you've no idea whether it'll be the fuck of your life or a complete wash-out. As I've said, usually it's the latter, but like a drug addict, you almost inevitably keep going back for more.

I think my own motivation is a selfish need to seek out kicks, put myself outside my comfort zone and feel the endorphin rush of a new and anonymous encounter. And I don't think having such a drive for sexual thrills is an entirely uncommon thing though. I remember being told about Russian Roulette Parties while on a visit to New Orleans. At these, perfectly healthy people would, just for the thrill and danger, indulge in unprotected orgies with other people known to be infected with HIV. I mean, how fucked up is that? When I compare myself to people like that, I'm tempted to think of myself as a totally normal, restrained and balanced human being. Well, I probably wouldn't go that far, but I think you catch my drift. There are obviously different levels to hedonism, and while being a thrill-seeker means I put myself around a bit, I still don't want to die as a consequence. Blondie helped me realise that. Dying is a bit too much out of my comfort zone.

chapter 14
more drugs, prison and
samuel l jackson

As far as drugs go, I'm quite ambivalent towards what I feel about the issue of legalisation. I think you should go either one way or the other – completely legalise everything, or adopt a no-tolerance policy and crack down on all illicit substances. At the moment, in England, the laws are applied with discretion – it's a bit wishy washy, with some local authorities turning a blind eye towards the possession of small amounts of drugs for personal use. Not all other European countries are as liberal, however, as I was to find out to my cost on a trip to Sweden.

I had been looking forward to the Stockholm leg of the *Sin Cities* tour, for the obvious reason that Swedish girls have a reputation for being among the best looking in Europe. Happily, I can now confirm that to be the case. Trust me, a night out in Stockholm can leave you with treasured images of some of the most stunning ladies in existence burnt onto your retinas for life. We had nearly finished our filming schedule, with just one more shoot before Aidan (director), Kate (assistant producer) and I were due to head off to Budapest. Everything had been going well and we were due a night out to let our hair down and pat ourselves on the back for a job well done.

We had a word with our fixer, translator and rock-chick-wannabe, Eva, to see if she could get her hands on some coke for us. She warned us that doing drugs in Sweden wasn't the same as it was back in England. Drug use, we learnt, was more than just frowned upon – possession of small amounts of Class A drugs was considered a serious offence, often resulting in a big fine or even a jail sentence. After thinking for a matter of seconds, we went full steam ahead.

'No problem, we'll be extra careful, here's the money, let's go and buy some drugs.'

A few hours and plenty of drinks later and we were doing gear off a car bonnet in full view of anyone and everyone. Not a good idea. When Eva saw what we were doing, she freaked out and rounded on us, saying we needed to be far more discreet or we would get into some serious shit. Fair enough, we said, as we headed off to a nightclub. Sometime later, I was in my usual messy state, but was keen to carry on the festivities with a heady mix of beers and bugle. I was making regular visits to the toilets to rack up a line or two, and had successfully demolished about half of my supply. I was just about to go for some more when Kate stopped me and asked if she could have some. After suggesting she wait for a couple of minutes and then come into the men's toilets, I headed off and cut out two lines of Bolivian go-fast, one for me and one for her. Then, as arranged, Kate knocked on the door of the cubicle. I opened up and handed her a rolled-up note to sort herself out. However, just as she was about to dive in and toot, the door to the toilet opened up again. Who the fuck was this? Then, a voice began to speak in Swedish, and with no small sense of dread I recognised one word from what was said: 'Police'.

'Fuck' was the next word that sprang to mind. I turned around as the police officer moved forward to take in the full picture. Without thinking, I immediately dabbed an outstretched finger over the last line and then shoved it in my mouth: a pretty stupid thing to do considering I was well and truly busted. At the time, though, my mind was so parched of sense that I was just thinking it would be a shame to waste a perfectly decent line. I was ushered out of the toilet and saw there were two more policemen waiting outside the door. As they led us out through the nightclub and into a kitchen area of an adjoining restaurant. I quickly whispered to Kate that I would carry the can for this. If she was asked anything about where we had got the gack from, then I wanted her to deny any knowledge and just say that I had given her a line and that was that. The last thing I wanted was for Eva and Aidan, who by this time had gone back to the hotel to bed, to get involved and be implicated in what had been our stupid mistake.

Next, we were searched and my remaining bit of cocaine was placed in a plastic bag on a table. I remember feeling some sense of relief that my left-over stash was so pitiful. Surely this was a cut-and-dried case of a minimal amount of possession (probably less than half a gram) for personal use and I would be let off with a slap on the wrist and a warning. The first indication that this was not to be the case was when more officers entered the room, followed by a man who was obviously a big noise in the Swedish police. This was looking ominous: Eva's words of warning were coming back to haunt us.

After some questioning, we were left to stew for a few

minutes. As far as I could make out from the police conversations, the cops were having a discussion about what had happened and they were now deciding whether to pursue the case or just let us go. Then the head honcho walked towards me, stopped and looked me up and down.

'Take off your glasses,' he ordered.

I knew what he was doing: checking me out to see how fucked up I was. I took my glasses off, praying that my eyes weren't in their usual unhealthy reddish state of disrepair. The Swedish Commandant leaned towards me and stared directly into my eyes. Unfortunately for me, it was not a pretty sight. Two pupils the size of saucers had sealed our fate – I was 100 percent wired.

'Take them down to the station,' he barked.

Kate and I were each bundled into a car and driven down to the police station. Bollocks. It was now well into the early hours of the morning. I had already written off any chance we might have had to complete our filming programme later on that day – instead I was now focusing on whether we could get out of our pickle in time to catch a flight to Budapest in 36 hours' time. If we missed it, we would fuck up the entire filming schedule for the next show and possibly the one after that. With people and locations already booked and confirmed, missing the flight would have major financial implications for the budget and possibly even for our jobs: this was a big fucking deal.

When we arrived at the station, we were kept apart and were taken to separate holding cells. Being imprisoned is a pretty rank experience at the best of times, but when you've been drowning in alcohol and stuffing drugs up your nose in the preceding six hours, it's a very dark and depressing way to suffer a comedown. Sitting on a hard concrete bed behind bars and worrying about whether my mistake was going to have serious repercussions for work was starting to give me a belting hangover. I must have been left for around four or five hours before the door was finally unlocked and I was led upstairs to be questioned. I sat down opposite the investigating officer who started asking me where I'd got the drugs. The truth was that we had driven to an apartment block somewhere on the outskirts of town, and handed our fixer the cash while she went upstairs to do the deal.

At this point I remember thinking back to a friend of mine who had filmed a documentary series in Miami with drugs squad officers. He'd told me that during interrogations, officers would look to see whether the suspects' eyes would veer to the left or the right while they replied to questioning: if they looked to the left (the creative side of the brain) they were more likely to be talking shit; if they looked to the right (the memory side), they were likely to be telling the truth. The problem was that in my mashed-up state I couldn't remember which side was which! Should I look left or right? Oh bollocks! I decided to hedge my bets, and resolved to look neither left nor right but stare straight into the eyes of my questioner.

'I bought them off some guy on the street,' I said. That should work.

'That's what you normally do is it, you just buy drugs off some random person off the street? Is that what you do in London?'

'Yes.'

'I don't believe you. Are you telling the truth?'

'Yes.' Eyes front.

'How often do you take drugs?'

'Not very often.' Eyes front.

'Do you want to change your mind and start telling me the truth? Tell me what really happened. We need to know where you bought the drugs.'

'I've told you the truth,' I insisted. 'I left the bar, went outside and someone asked me if I wanted to buy some coke and I bought it off him.'

'What did he look like?'

Man, it was a nightmare. I rattled off some vague description, quite possibly in a very unconvincing fashion. I was, after all, still feeling the effects of the night. Then I was asked what I was doing in Stockholm.

'We're making a television programme.'

'What about?'

'Er, it's like a late-night show about nightlife... adult behaviour,' I said.

This grabbed his attention. 'Adult behaviour?'

'Well, sex, I suppose.'

'You're filming pornography?'

Shit; this was starting to go wrong. That's not the reaction I usually get. Not only did he think I was a junkie, but now a porn baron.

'Er, not exactly...'

I rambled on about what we had been filming, but my explanations as to why we had spent the previous day filming a seventy-year-old man, Hans, birching the bare backsides of his harem of young female companions can't have made much sense. Some more questioning, some awkward silences and we were done. I was taken back downstairs and the door to my cell banged shut behind me. I wondered how Kate was feeling and whether she'd stuck to our story without getting the other members of the team involved. Fingers crossed. All kinds of scenarios were rushing through my mind. I'd all but lost hope that I'd be on that flight to Budapest and resigned myself to the fact that the schedule was well and truly down the shitter. Then the door to my cell opened up again and I was summoned back upstairs.

I sat down in front of the investigating officer.

170

'Mr Hames, we went back and searched your hotel room. Could you explain what these items are please?'

On the table before me were placed a 12-inch double-ended dildo, a plastic mould of my own penis, a bunch of small birch branches tied together and some porn DVDs. Oh Christ! This wasn't looking good. To make matters worse, it was now apparent they were taking this case sufficiently seriously to go and search my hotel room. My explanation, which was entirely truthful, was that when I go on my travels, I like to keep mementos of the trip – the double-ended dildo had been given to me by the owner of a sex shop, the cock mould had been made as part of filming that week in Stockholm, the branches were a souvenir from yesterday's visit to Hans, our new favourite OAP practitioner of S&M, while the DVDs had been a gift from a porn star who we had filmed some weeks earlier. I didn't see it as a problem.

The policeman looked at me carefully and then asked me again if I had come to his country to make 'sex films'. Well, even if I had, I wasn't convinced that that was exactly illegal, but rather than cause a scene, I explained that we were making a 'comedy' television programme. I added that I would appreciate it if we could get this whole thing cleared up as soon as possible because I was planning on leaving the country in less than 20 hours to go filming in Budapest.

'Tell us the truth and you can leave. Do you want to tell the truth?'

It was like being in a bad police drama. The porno props just turned it into a farce and I knew I'd probably start laughing if I wasn't so bothered about the flight. Then I'd really be in the shit.

'I have told you the truth,' I lied. 'I can't tell you anything else, unless you want me to start making things up.'

With that I was led back to my cell. Time started to catch up with me. I hadn't slept for ages, my head was hurting from a full-blown hangover and I'd been given nothing to eat to help sober me up. My only respite was a solitary cigarette, bizarrely smoked on the roof of the building with a policeman supervising my every move. A few more hours of mind-numbing boredom in my cell followed before I was interrupted. This time, my interrogator walked in and told me to stay seated on the bed.

'So you want to leave here and get your flight to Budapest, do you?'

'Yep.'

'Well then, you'd better get your story straight,' he demanded. 'If you tell me the truth then you can leave very soon. If you don't, then you may be here for a few days, possibly more. At the moment your story doesn't correspond with that of your friend, Kate. I believe she is telling the truth. Do you want to tell me where you really bought the drugs or are you going to keep insisting that you bought them off the street?'

Oh, arse. Had Kate cracked and ended up spilling the beans or was this a bluff? Fuck it, I was gonna stick to my story. I'd seen enough bad police dramas to be able to play them at their own game.

'Well, I've no idea what else you've been told; all I know is that I was telling you the truth.'

'OK. Stay here.'

Where else would I be going?

'Don't I get to see a lawyer or anything?' I asked him. 'I've been here for ages now.'

'No. Wait here.'

Shit. A couple more hours passed. Then another officer entered my cell. This time it looked like things were finally moving on towards my release. I was told I could leave if I paid a fine of somewhere in the region of two grand. Yikes! That seemed a bit fucking steep for having less than half a gram of cocaine. Still, I didn't really have much choice: it was either that or completely screw up the *Sin Cities* filming schedule and lose my job. After agreeing to their ransom, and somewhat dubiously, I was then taken out of the station and driven around town to use my credit card to take out money from various cash machines. I was a tad suspicious that these funds were going to end up straight in the pockets of the cops, but to be honest I didn't really give a shit – as long as they let me out, I was happy. Luckily, I had the money in my account, and when we returned to the police station I was asked to sign a statement. With no knowledge of Swedish and no lawyer with me, I had absolutely no idea what I was signing; but bearing in mind it was now just a matter of a few hours before I was due to catch a flight to Budapest, I signed it regardless.

'Thank you, Mr Hames. You are free to go now.'

Thank fuck for that. I walked out of the police station, turned the corner, hailed the first cab that came down the street and headed back to the hotel. Hopping out of the taxi, I saw Kate standing outside the hotel. As I walked towards her I gave her the 'V' for victory sign and shouted out in triumph.

'Hey Kate, you never can say you've done a city until you've been arrested. Stockholm – we did it!'

As I drew closer, however, I noticed with alarm that Kate was in floods of tears.

'Oh Kate, it's alright. Come on. We're out now... it's fine. What's up?'

It turned out that Kate had ended up telling the police about the involvement of our fixer, Eva, in helping us to buy the drugs. The police had arrested both her and Aidan, who at the time had been asleep in his hotel bed. They'd been taken down to the police station for questioning and each and every one of us had been fined £2000. Aidan was obviously not happy. Fuck! One small mistake had screwed things up big style. I went upstairs to see him and found him packing up his bags for the trip. Aidan was, thankfully, incredibly calm about the whole thing and told me not to worry too much about it but just to get my shit together because we were leaving for the airport in less than two hours.

'Don't worry, Ash,' he said. 'If you live by the sword, you die by the sword.'

If I ever get rich I will happily pay Aidan's fine for him. As things stand, I ended up paying Eva's fine for her, and half of Kate's on top of my own. All in all, that works out at £5000 for a night out on the town in Stockholm – a pretty expensive evening's entertainment! And I didn't even get laid. Sod that for a laugh.

Aidan, I think, had been so chilled out about the whole episode because I suspect he was quite used to dealing with drugs and the risk of trouble they can bring. Confirmation of his familiarity with the more illicit side of life came on our last week of filming together in Ibiza. On our first afternoon there, Aidan and I approached a dealer on the beach outside Bora Bora, a well known hotspot for buying drugs.

'Alright mate,' Aidan began.

'OK fellas, what can I get you?'

'What have you got?' replied Aidan.

'Look, you just tell me what you want and I'll sort it out for you. What do you want?'

'Everything you've got,' came Aidan's reply.

I looked over at him. Everything?! Jesus, it looked like Aidan was up for a big one.

'Well, listen lads, I've got about thirty pills and six grams of coke.'

Aidan didn't miss a beat. 'We'll take them. How

174

much?'

That's a lot of drugs. With the transaction complete, a 48-hour-binge later and there was a fair amount of chaos to deal with. Within the first 12 hours I got off my face and achieved the near impossible by getting thrown out of Space nightclub after walking out of the toilet with a bleeding nose. Having failed to make it back to the hotel by the end of the following day, Aidan phoned the production company back in England to report that I'd gone missing and asked if they'd heard from me. They hadn't. The truth was that I'd spent another 24 hours in another nightclub, Underground, where I'd been the first in and the last to leave. I had then, somehow or other, ended up on a beach miles from the nearest town with a girl I met in a nearby car park who had facial tattoos and a tattooed bolt of lightning pointing down to her crotch. Drugs, you understand, lead to that kind of mayhem.

Despite what you've read, my use of illegal intoxicants has, in the main, been fairly infrequent. For me, it was predominantly bingeing on the odd occasion when I fancied a blow-out. As someone who suffers from acute hangovers, the option of doing drugs and alcohol on a daily basis is an exceptionally bad idea. Nowadays if you were to catch me using drugs, it would be a very rare slip-up.

I think society does get it right by saying drugs are bad for you – they can sometimes be a complete fucking nightmare. But, for the occasional user at least, it's difficult to deny that they can also sometimes be fun. In my experience, they're usually a combination of the two. But increasingly as you get older, and as ignorance and complacency are replaced with a healthier dose of cynicism, you find they are way more hassle than they're worth. In fact, as I look back, I think even the 'fun', as

I've described it, was a twisted, slightly vacuous and meaningless kind of fun. Drugs, you see, have no depth or feeling to them, they're just... surface. They are like the one-night stand that you always regret the next day.

It's also no secret that drugs have a devastating cost to other people who you just don't think about when you're planning a Friday night bender with a couple of grams of the white stuff. Recently, I was lucky enough to go to Colombia, a country which is notorious as the cradle of the cocaine industry. While there, I visited the military hospital and met some of the men who had been seriously maimed and disfigured by the cocaine wars. I left feeling incredibly guilty about how my own usage had indirectly contributed to their pain and injury. Before going to Colombia, I'd seldom bothered to think beyond my own enjoyment – but I have since reflected on my visit there a lot, and it's had a major effect on my behaviour. Drugs are out: I'd much rather just get pissed instead.

Colombia was not the only place in the world where I was to discover that drugs are part and parcel of the fabric of society. I remember some years before, when I arrived in Jamaica on my *Sin Cities* tour of duty, I checked into my hotel room and decided to order myself a sandwich from room service. When the waiter arrived, he put the sandwich down on my side-table and then looked up at me and asked if he could get me anything else. I instantly recognised 'the look'.

'What can you get me?' I asked.

'Weed, coke, girls. Whatever you want.'

'Hmmm, I tell you what, can you get me two grams of coke, please?'

Minutes later, I was sniffing the strongest cocaine I'd ever had. This was room service with a difference. As the stop-off point for drugs headed between South America and the USA and Europe, the drugs available in Jamaica are very pure and uncut. This can be a good thing and also a very bad thing. The good thing being that after a couple of lines I was as high as a kite – the bad thing being that a top-brass production bod (for the sake of this little episode, let's call him the boss) was flying over from England on a mission to check that we were doing our jobs properly. And if I was ripped to the tits on grade A gack, then it could probably have been a sign that all wasn't well on set. It got worse: the boss was due to land in just a few hours time. Cue drug paranoia. If I'd known this at the time, maybe I wouldn't have had so much toot.

Upon arrival, the boss invited me, Denise and John – the director – out for a meal. All three of us had by now blasted our way through my stash of gear and, by the time we sat down to eat, were left looking somewhat worse for wear. Sometimes you consume the drugs; at other times, they consume you – this was one of those latter occasions. The meal wasn't a complete disaster, but not far off either.

'So John, how are things going?'

John is staring into the distance, completely monged-out, his eyes boggling and semi-focused on a point around a thousand miles away.

'Eh? Yeah, pretty good, pretty good.' He stops talking and takes a swig of beer.

Silence follows. A look of alarm rises on the face of the boss.

'OK... and how are you Denise?'

Denise glanced over with one eye looking one way and the other somewhere else entirely. Denise, as well as being an extremely resourceful crew member, also had a huge capacity for drugs. Understand, this was a girl who had won 'Blagger of the Year' on the Ibiza party circuit for two years in succession. Yet despite her notable track record of debauchery, it appeared that even she was having trouble keeping a straight face after her recent intake of Jamaican Class As. That's putting it mildly – she was completely lop-sided, gurning like an absolute maniac and looking, frankly, quite scary. In answer to 'How are you?' she launched into a drug-fuelled mono-logue of total nonsense, leaving our boss looking totally non-plussed. Fuck. I was next.

'And Ashley, are you happy with the show?'

The truth was that things hadn't been going all that great – a few of the shoots had fallen through and, what we were actually filming wasn't exactly breaking any new ground. Naturally I decided to lie and tell him the opposite.

'Yeah, it's all good. No worries there.'

I'm sure he'd had better dinner conversations than that in his life and I suspect he was wishing that a) he'd eaten alone and b) he'd stayed in England.

The following day, with the three of us having strug-gled to get any sleep whatsoever, the boss accompanied us to work. Fortunately for us, John had the constitution of an ox and managed to pull the proverbial cat out off the bag. John's eyes may have been red-raw, Denise's voice a tad croaky, and my general appearance closer to a street urchin than a presenter, but when John called wrap, we knew we had another class show in the bag. As the boss made his welcome return to the airport, we collapsed in relief and headed back to the hotel for some more room service. But this time, I ignored 'the look' and went for a sandwich instead. You always know where you are with a BLT.

A visit to South Africa opened my eyes further to the potency and price difference of drugs overseas. And when they're cheap you tend to do too much of them – at least that was our experience when the *Sin Cities* gang spent a night out in a strip club in Cape Town. This particular evening ended up with me, Aidan and Kate teamed up for a memorable drug-fuelled night of debauchery. When we heard that coke was only about £15 a gram compared to the usual £50 back home, we knew we were set for a shocker.

We had originally gone to a strip joint, Mavericks, to check it out as a possible venue for filming, but when the owner offered us some drinks on the house, our initial visit began to morph into one long stop-over, and before long our table was overflowing with booze, bottles and ashtrays. When it became clear that drugs were also doing the rounds, we got stuck in and soon we were game on for another night of carnage. With his venue as a potential place for filming, the owner was being especially nice to us, giving us top-notch VIP treatment, including access to a private toilet. There, we could get loaded at our convenience without the danger of bumping into any other punters. A strip club is a great place for a couple of coked-up lads, and soon Aidan and I had found some excellent company in the form of several sultry strippers dancing seductively around our table and waving their boobs in our face.

Kate, meanwhile, had found something equally attractive in the shape of none other than American actor, Samuel L. Jackson. Jackson was in town to do some filming himself, and Kate, on spotting him, ran up to him for a chat. I glanced over to catch her in mid-flow, eyes ablaze and gnashing her teeth, frantically declaring her undying admiration to a somewhat quizzical-looking Jackson. A few minutes later things got even more surreal, as she clambered up on stage and treated us all to a stage dance... although I suspect it was intended purely for her new Hollywood buddy.

Despite being equally off his face, Aidan was

nevertheless enjoying great success in chatting up a very foxy young stripper, while I tried to focus my attentions on a buxom bar-girl who was keen on showing me a better view of her ample curves. Sure enough, Aidan and I later took our new-found friends back to our rented apartment where we were given a good old fashioned seeing to.

By morning, I'd succeeded in getting absolutely no sleep whatsoever and my jittery state was made worse by the knowledge that we were supposed to be doing some more filming later that day. I looked in the mirror – not a pretty sight. I was horribly pasty and my eyes looked on the verge of bleeding. This was what people mean when they say 'a face like death warmed up'. Fuck – I was in no state to do anything, let alone embarrass myself on camera again. When Aidan woke up I asked him how he was feeling, wondered if I should come clean and let him know I was somewhat off my game. When he confessed to still feeling battered himself, I admitted to him that I hadn't slept a wink. He immediately burst out laughing and I gave a huge sigh of relief – the last thing you want is for someone to give you grief when you're feeling a bit edgy. Kate, however, not having done much coke before, was struggling with the comedown, and when I asked her if she was OK, looked close to tears. The huge downside to drugs is the depression and paranoia that soak into your soul the following day and it's quite common to fall to pieces. Kate, it was clear, was having one of these moments. I had a word with Aidan and we discussed whether we should bother with any filming. Trouble is, we were due to leave the next day and we hadn't done anything near enough to make a full programme. We decided the best thing to do was to try and arrange a shoot rather than all sit around feeling sorry for ourselves – it would be far better to get stuck into some work, all pitch in together, forget the drug-induced pain we were now suffering from and see if we could get ourselves through it. Trouble was, we hadn't yet locked down anything to film. That was something we were supposed to have sorted out the previous day when, instead, we had ended up getting mashed. Luckily, I then had a bit of a brainwave.

'Hey, how about we hire some of those strippers from the club last night, get them out onto a speedboat and see if I can guess their bra sizes… that would be fun.'

It wasn't exactly ground-breaking, but Aidan liked the idea. We were in business, and within a few hours we were racing around the ocean on a speedboat enjoying the company of some all-too-familiar faces. After being treated to seeing all the girls in bras, then topless, I ended up getting five out the eleven bra sizes spot on – considering the state I was in and the fact that I could scarcely see out from behind the darkest pair of shades I could find, I rate that as a damn fine achievement. And it certainly helped make me feel a lot better. I'd recommend it to anyone as a hangover cure.

chapter 15
gord almighty

My rather wired existence during this time had been yet another wake up call to the fact that drugs and I weren't exactly the best of bed fellows. All they seemed to do was either lead me into trouble, or leave me with no sleep and a throbbing headache. I needed to start channelling my energies into work, rather than on getting high. Bad hangovers, it seemed, were now my constant companion on the *Sin Cities* road. That needed changing.

I remember arriving somewhere in America after a heavy few days' partying and I was so drained that when the customs officer asked me where I was travelling from, my mind was a complete blank. I stopped and tried to gather my thoughts for a moment. Where had I just come from? Canada? No. Japan? No. Shit. That's weird; I had no recollection at all.

I turned around and saw Denise in the queue behind me; 'Hey Denise, where have we just come from?' I asked.

Denise looked at me, couldn't quite believe what she

was hearing, and quietly informed me we had just been in Mexico. Oh yeah. Mexico. That's the one. Fucking hell! We'd been there for well over a week and I'd forgotten all about it. In fact, Mexico had been an amazing time for us – aside from filming naked deep sea diving, semi-naked wrestling and some variety of tantric sex, it was also one of the first times in my life where I felt a little bit famous. *Sin Cities* gets a regular viewing on FX Channel to millions of viewers throughout the whole of South America, so I was often approached by people who had seen me on television. It was odd walking around town and being approached by fans of the show and being called Mr Sin Cities. The novelty of being known was nice, even better was the fact that drinks would be shoved my way in virtually every bar we walked into. It was also satisfying to know that people were enjoying the programmes and that my regular moments of pain and humiliation did at least have some kind of audience around the world.

Bearing in mind the novelty of finding myself to be an almost bona fide celebrity there, it was strange to think I could have forgotten I had even been in the country. I imagine I was still suffering some kind of after-effect from a night out in Rosarito a few days earlier where I'd snorted some very dodgy crystal meth-amphetamines, downed a shed-load of gold-leaf tequila, and ended up in the hotel swimming pool fully-clothed.

Still a bit fried, but holding it together the best we could, we arrived in the States on our usual mission – to investigate sex – which in America, as I was about to discover, is akin to opening up Pandora's Box. The US is, quite simply, home to some of the most staggeringly bizarre and extreme forms of sexuality on the planet. That much was obvious the moment I arrived in Seattle to visit the House of Gord, home to my fellow countryman and all-round English eccentric, Jeff Gord. This place was a little bit fucking weird to say the least. Jeff is a man who specialises in what's known as forniphilia. Put simply, forniphilia is a type of bondage which aims to transform women into pieces of furniture. *Yes, way.*

Now, I have heard of and seen some pretty weird shit in my life, but this really takes the prize. Jeff had, via an inventive use of various accoutrements, turned women into tables, chairs, stools, lawn sprinklers and lamps. When I met him it was early in the morning on a very cold wintry day. We'd been travelling for well over a day, stayed in a shitty motel in the middle of nowhere and I had woke up in a terrible mood – the last thing I wanted to do was prat around with what I assumed would be some dodgy weirdo who straps women up, sticks a light on their head and then calls them a human lamp. Jeff, however, as I was to find out, had far loftier intentions. While freely admitting that what he did may be deemed by some to be wacko, freakish or just plain perverse, Jeff claimed his work to be of genuine artistic merit. By the end of my time with him, I was inclined to agree.

Jeff is an entirely non-descript man – mid forties, unkempt hair, glasses... but what he does is nothing short of extraordinary. Upon our arrival he explained that for his first demonstration he'd make one of his stable of willing participants into a car emblem. Confused? OK, you know those Mercedes signs they have sticking up at the front of the vehicle? Well, Jeff's plan was to strap a girl onto the front of his truck in the same pose. Yep, I know, but bear with me.

Having painstakingly built a complicated-looking contraption attached to the bonnet, Jeff invited his rubber-clad model of the day, Ceci, to step on board where she was promptly gagged, rotated and cocooned in several layers of cling-film. With both of her legs splayed at 45 degrees, Jeff then proceeded to attach a pulsating dildo beneath her and a set of electrodes to her crotch, all of which, he promised, was designed to stimulate her and send her into a frenzy of multiple orgasms.

With Ceci wrapped up like a supermarket sandwich and firmly strapped to the front of his truck, Jeff jumped into the driver's seat and proceeded to hurtle around the grounds of his house as his truck's now ecstatic appendage screamed out in pleasure. Screeching to a halt, he de-gagged Ceci who immediately begged for more of the same, having claimed to have already reached orgasm several times. Determined however, to show off his full repertoire, Jeff unravelled his all-too-willing accomplice and led her inside the House of Gord. She was now, he revealed, set to become a human chandelier. Suffice to say that after much preparation and to general all-round astonishment from me and the crew, Ceci was invited to spread her legs, then attached to a metal frame and an automatic winch, and hoisted up to the ceiling where she was suspended in mid-air. Jeff stood watching, near-tears of joy in his eyes, as he then applied the coup de grâce, flicking a light switch to reveal his new, and I have to say, quite stunning creation. I was struck by the incredible lengths Jeff was prepared to go to in order to get his sexual kicks. For Jeff and his cohorts, there's a huge amount of time, money and technical expertise put into taking their particular fetish scene to the next level. Rope suspension, electric play, mummification: these are not things you chance upon – they take hours of study, dedication and skill.

At no point in the proceedings, however, did it appear that Jeff was necessarily aroused by what he was doing. He was not, in other words, stroking his knob and groaning with pleasure while his new masterpiece made its entrance into the world. But, I thought afterwards, he must be getting something out of it. I mean, why else do it? Why invest so much effort into something that doesn't appear to end in sexual climax? But then again, how the fuck would you even get gratification from turning an attractive girl into what is essentially a glorified light-bulb? Was Jeff a nutty sexual professor, inventing madcap ways to keep his interest in sex alive? He may well be that, and more besides. But why did he turn to forniphilia? Transforming women into furniture is more than just a little surreal. I have to be honest; I didn't quite get it. I could just put it down to the behaviour of a slightly mad Englishman, but was I missing a trick here? So anyway, I decided to do some extra research on Jeff to try and find out what motivated him to do what he did.

What I read on his website opened my eyes to what lies behind this kind of bondage play. There, and at some length, Jeff describes forniphilia as 'an expression of man's desire to render a powerful and dangerous adversary to the role of utility item. By relegating them to an item of furniture that can be used and enjoyed at leisure and in complete safety, we can achieve that goal.' What he's saying here is that it is in man's nature to control and conquer. By using our physical strength we can overcome, but never truly win. So, reduce a woman to a usable object and she becomes so damned sexually alluring that she has you by the balls so to speak. Jeff would urge you to try sitting on a human female chair, with a human female table, and a human female foot stool. Only then, would he say, you really stop caring about the battle of the sexes.

Fair enough, but what about the women involved? I wondered. What do they get out of it? I was told that true bondage-loving ladies love the attention it brings them and they thrive on the power over their male counterparts. Jeff's art is about treating women with the respect they deserve, providing a safe environment, keeping it consensual and caring about their wellbeing. He is always sincere and honest with his subjects and this completely flies in the face of so many people's preconceptions, including my own, about bondage. When you see a man tying a woman up, or in Jeff's case, turning her into a chair, lampshade or bedside table, it's difficult to get away from the suspicion that it is some kind of misogynistic practice that denigrates women. Jeff, however, insists this is not the case at all.

'One must never ever underestimate the female of the species. Respect them and treat them right, that is the key. One of the first issues you must attend to is to get the message over to a woman that, although she may be bound, objectified, whatever you want to call it, a bound bondage playmate holds all the cards. The bound woman becomes not an object of ridicule, but an object of immense power in the eyes of a bondage master.'

Fair point. For him, it's a catch-22 situation that he's never managed to resolve, nor does he really want to. His rationale is simple: if you don't please her, she will never want to play again. If you hurt her or betray her trust by refusing to release her when she uses the safe word, you are toast. A quaint way of putting it is that the true bondage master becomes the moth fluttering around the flickering candle flame... treat the flame with respect or you will be burned up.

I think on another level it's very simple – aside from loving bondage-play, Jeff also considers himself something of an artist who, while transforming his subjects from normal human beings into everyday objects, thinks what he does has a certain aesthetic beauty. And I would agree with him. But what he does is also highly sexualised: rubber suits, mouth gags and dildos all add colour to what is, essentially, an advanced form of bondage. When we were filming with him, I asked Jeff to explain his fetish further.

'Ashley,' he answered, 'at the end of the day, what this is about is fun. Sex is supposed to be fun.' And then, with his tongue wedged firmly in his cheek, he added, 'If it's not fun, it's rape!'

That may be a joke of questionable taste but I can see what he's driving at. Besides, I've always been struck by how seriously some people take sex, as if the act of fornication is something not to be tampered with. Although he took great care in what he did, like me, Jeff appears anxious to dispel the reverence surrounding coitus. So often, the subject of sex and sexuality is spoken of in hushed tones, as if it's a dirty word, like it's naughty, taboo and ever so slightly sacred. For Jeff, sex was to be cherished and explored, and forniphilia was his way of doing that. And I for one won't knock him for that. In fact, I think it sometimes takes real balls to put your kink out there in the public arena, especially one as bizarre as forniphilia. If, like Jeff, you go off the beaten sexual track towards a more unconventional kind of sexual fulfilment, you may find yourself part of a sexual minority. And, like all minorities, you automatically run the risk of being victimised and scorned. Like all prejudices, I put this down to other people's fear of the unknown. And just as I had been similarly guilty of setting out for the House of Gord with a negative and cynical attitude, what I saw at firsthand helped me bury those prejudices and accept what Jeff did for what it was – a lot of fun. If sex was a music scene, Jeff would be the Johnny Rotten, the punk destroyer of accepted sexual values and standards, and for that I salute him. Me? I'll still settle for the sophistication of a snog and a blowjob on a Saturday night. Please.

chapter 16
double penetration

Our recent visit to the House of Gord had the benefit of allowing us a couple of days off in nearby Seattle, one of the best cities in the world for a night's entertainment. After filming, we headed for the city centre, where I successfully indulged my own particular fetish of getting hammered and passing out.

Life on the road with *Sin Cities*, as you've probably gathered by now, was a little bit like being in a slightly dysfunctional rock 'n' roll band, with all the incumbent highs and lows. However, I hoped that by the time we headed back to Europe I would give myself some breathing space and try and steer clear from too much self-harm. I'm not saying I wanted to just eat salad and drink water, but I was well aware that drug and alcohol abuse (never call it misuse) meant I was in danger of slipping off the tracks and spinning out of control. Sadly, the omens weren't good: Amsterdam was our next port of call, and as far as sin cities go, it's up there with the best of them. One more for the road, then?

Unsurprisingly, due to a seriously high level of intoxication, I honestly cannot recall a great deal from my time there. I have hazy memories of going out on an all-nighter, getting spliffed-up and then being filmed in the town square completely incapable of forming a coherent sentence. Despite not being able to communicate beyond a slur and a mumble, we still resolved to keep our filming appointment later that morning with a group of naked darts players. I didn't hit a double all day – apart from those available from the bar, obviously. I have vague memories of downing pints, pouring spirits over my pubic hair, setting a match to them and seeing my entire crotch lit up like a Christmas tree. And that's about it. Darts? Been there, done that, filmed the wet T-shirt.

It seemed I kept making personal promises to calm down and kept breaking them. It was a worrying pattern. After the carnage of Amsterdam, I yet again resolved to try and concentrate a little bit more on work and try and stop getting into the scrapes that seemed to be rapidly forming a regular part of our evening's entertainment. I was slipping into a seriously debauched lifestyle. It was time to pull in the reigns and grow up a little bit. Besides, I didn't want to end up dead or in prison again just yet. I was hopeful that our time in Eastern Europe could be the fresh start I needed.

And so, another promise was made. After getting off the plane in the Czech capital, Prague, we were greeted at the airport by our translator.

'Hi fellas, welcome to Prague,' he began. 'What can I sort you out with? Do you want coke, ecstasy, speed? Girls? You want girls? I can get you some great chicks if you like.'

Oh Christ. Thirty-six hours later I had taken a mountain of drugs, slept with two prostitutes and lost my entire week's wages at the casino. And so, another promise was broken. Great self-discipline, Ash. Prague, it has to be said, was a complete blast from start to finish. The city is well known as a haven for stag parties, and by the end of my week there I could understand why. On our first night, we headed out into town and found a bar that specialised in setting cocktail drinks on fire. A few mouth blisters was a small price to pay for the amusement of seeing my then-director (Duncan again) being sick in the gutter outside. Despite such light relief, I was desperate to get some sleep and eventually, as dawn was breaking, we made it back to the hotel. Scarcely had my eyelids met than I was being woken up by Denise. With close to zero kip there was another full day of filming ahead of us. Nightmare. We packed, checked, re-checked and were off.

'Where are we filming?' I asked Denise.

'In a brothel,' she replied.

The nightmare swiftly turned into a wet dream. A day of filming in K5, one of Prague's most notorious brothels, complete with themed rooms, two huge bars and well over thirty working girls, was followed by yet another twelve hours in K5, where, not to put too fine a point on it, we did absolutely no work at all but made the best use of all the available facilities. The next day, replete with hangover and regrets, I spoke to Duncan, bemoaning the fact that I had quite literally spunked all my cash away.

'Mate,' he replied, 'don't worry about it — that's the reason you got the job. If you weren't like that, you wouldn't be getting paid and wouldn't have the money to blow in the first place.'

Hearing that made all my morally dubious behaviour seem entirely justifiable, but it did get me thinking that I should put something away for a rainy day. That, unfortunately, has never happened. I invariably return to England from my working stints abroad completely skint.

But let's just say that my memory wank bank makes me a multi-millionaire, of sorts.

Prague – as well as Eastern Europe in general – is renowned for being a haven for porn directors, mainly because the girls tend to be extremely good-looking and are paid considerably less than their English or American counterparts. Bizarrely, one of the first porn shoots I ever attended was filmed slap bang in the centre of Prague, next door to a coffee shop. The section given over to filming also hosted the toilets to the café, so if any customers were caught short, they were also treated to some full-on hardcore porn action.

As we walked into the café I was introduced to the director – a very sultry Italian lady in her thirties. So much for the cliché of porn being the domain of dodgy old men in raincoats. She then invited me to take part in her movie – she wanted me to approach a couple who would be having sex on a table, get 'little Ashley' out and masturbate while watching them. *What?!* I had scarcely lost my porn virginity, and now I was being beckoned to knock one out on camera! Luckily, I managed to convince her that my acting abilities weren't yet up to scratch, and instead I took my place behind the scenes and watched the action unfurl.

I suppose today, having racked up three series of *Sin Cities*, I find a porn shoot no more outrageous than a slice of cheesecake. But back in those early days, it was a peculiar experience. I'm not sure what I expected but, with the odd notable exception, it certainly wasn't a sexual turn-on. Nor was it particularly glamorous or thrilling. It ain't Hollywood, put it that way. Instead, it's a crazy mix of the clinical and chaotic, the bizarre and mundane. I think above all, what I'll always remember from being on the set of porn films is the smell and sounds as well as the actual sights that you see. The smell is a mixture of slightly overpowering perfume mixed in with sweat and other more intimate bodily fluids. The sounds are a constant barrage of moans and groans, along with regular cries of feigned pleasure, moving on to orgasmic screams of ecstasy (and that was just the crew... b'boom, ching!). There were also a lot of stock phrases used by the girls, which, in no particular order went something like this:

1. Oooh yeah, put your cock in my pussy.
2. Oh my God, yes, oh my God!
3. Fuck me! That's it baby, fuck me now! Harder!
4. I love your big fat cock!
5. I want you to cum on my face.

Yeah, it's safe to say that this was a far cry from the phrases coming out of my own bedroom...

1. It's not very big is it?
2. Are you in yet?
3. Have you finished?
4. Can we try something other than missionary?
5. Don't call me, I'll call you.

Despite the often-predictable nature of most porn shoots, there were some occasions when being on set could really knock you for six. Budapest, for example, was home to my first experience of double penetration. For those who don't watch too much hardcore pornography, double penetration (or DP as it's known in the business) is one girl being fucked by two guys at once, with one cock in the front bottom, and one in the rear.

When we arrived on set, it was bustling with film crew sorting out lighting, props, and make-up. Naked male and female models were walking casually around as they waited to be told what to do and where to go. After meeting them all, we hung around for the action to unfold. And then it did. Action was called and they, indeed, needed no further encouragement. One couple were filmed having sex and then another strapping young lad joined in the action to make it a threesome. Before long, both of the boys were simultaneously having their way with the young actress. Physically, DP is quite a feat to achieve. I seem to remember that in this instance one of the lads was sat down on a sofa with his cock up the girl's more traditional orifice, while the other bloke was taking the less frequented route by straddling from behind. What I have no trouble remembering is the look on the girl's face as she relished the feeling of double delight – she quite obviously loved it.

I'm sure some of you are now thinking, 'Come on Ash, this is a porn flick, she was probably faking it.'

Well, I'm not so sure. Everyone seems far too hasty to insist it's ludicrous to suggest that porn stars could possibly enjoy their work. In a brutally exploitative industry, where actresses are used and abused to cater for misogynistic male fantasies, the reasoning goes: the girls have to be faking it. I'm not saying they're having multiple orgasms every time they set foot on set – they are after all, porn actresses. And sure, I have seen more than just the odd girl glaze over with boredom before turning it on, feigning ecstasy and yelping in delight for the benefit of the cameras. But take my word for it: many of the girls (and guys) do genuinely enjoy their work.

I think the reason many people find it difficult to believe that actors and actresses might enjoy their jobs is down to the constant labelling of a so-called 'exploitative sex industry'. I think there are undoubtedly people in positions of power who are out to exploit weak and vulnerable wannabes – but name me another industry where that isn't the case. The porn industry is really just like any other, with good and bad in equal measure. Of course there is a suspect side to porn, but in my experience, the media tend to focus unfairly on that side of it, to stereotype it as a world of fucked-up perverts, of predatory men exploiting underpaid and drug-addicted girls. I'm no mug though, and I'm fully aware that porn can sometimes get a bad press for a reason. So let's have a quick time-out here and take a closer look at the shadier aspects of the industry.

If you look at the actresses in the industry, some of them will start off with strict limits to what they will and won't do. Little by little, however, those limits, morals, principles, call them what you will, start getting eroded because word gets around that they won't do such and such a thing and directors will take the easy way out and just hire girls that do everything. The girl that starts off in the industry with strict limits – doing, say, just girl-on-girl lesbian films – may find herself, several years down the line, doing things like gang bangs and anal scenes – stuff that's a million miles away from her original plan. She's not necessarily being *coerced* into doing what she doesn't want to, but if she's hoping to make a successful living in the industry, then any limits she may have set will usually have to be thrown out of the window. If her survival in the industry means she has to do things like double vaginal (two penises in the vagina) or even double anal, then she may decide to do that, with all the health as well as moral issues that that incurs. And yes, in case you were wondering, double anal, double vaginal, you name it: they do it.

History also shows that the more hardcore the action becomes, the more the girls will turn to drugs, alcohol and tranquillisers as a means of dealing with their distress and discomfort. The way pornography is going, with ever more hardcore films being made to grab the attention of an increasingly saturated market, makes me think that a greater number of girls will find themselves in this situation. And that's an incredibly sad thing. Remember, we're now living in an age where you can download images and footage onto a mobile phone at the touch of a button. Because of that, millions more people are able to see porn on a regular basis. And they do: the demand is there. But in contemporary society, in order for it to have impact on a desensitised audience, it now has to shock. If it's not shocking, it won't create a buzz; it won't be seen and won't be financially viable. The effect this has is to encourage film-makers to push boundaries and in turn, for porn actresses (and, of course, actors) to do things they otherwise would have rejected as beyond the pale.

One indicator of how increased demand for the more outrageous, more extreme side of pornography has a knock-on effect within the industry can be seen in gang bang videos. Back in 1995, Annabel Chong set the world record for screwing the most number of men in a day – 251. That figure is a bit misleading – it's alleged that only around 70 men turned up and engaged in 251 'sex acts'. But whatever, it's still pretty far out. More significantly, the resulting film, *World's Biggest Gang Bang*, was one of the highest grossing porn videos of all time. That success and the wealth it generated led to a rush of similar films, and less than five years later, the world gang bang record held by the American porn starlet, Houston, stood at an incredible 620. Similarly, this was 620 'sex acts', not 620 individuals, with the numerous men being 'recycled' in order to get to the final figure. Again, it was the highest-selling video of the year.

What this illustrates is how consumer demand

continually ups the ante and drives market forces towards more extreme and shocking content. In five years' time what will that new figure be? Someone, somewhere, will be planning the first ever 1000 sex-partner gang-bang video release and will become an overnight millionaire. If we take it as a given that this is a dangerous, disturbing trend, then who is at fault here? The director and producers for making it? The porn star for consenting to it? Or us, the consumers for buying it? And where is porn headed? What's next? Surely they are all only supplying what the audience is demanding.

To help answer some of these questions, I got back in touch with an old friend. Laurien DuTremble is a well-established director who I filmed during a visit to Los Angeles. Married to porn star Taylor Wane, Laurien lives a stone's throw away from the heart of the porn industry in LA's San Fernando Valley. I asked him how things had changed since he had started out in the industry over twenty-five years ago.

His reply:

'When I first got into porn in the early 80s it was all controlled by the mob. It had more of a "family" feel to it than it does now. As "tame" as the filming was back then, it was still illegal to make it and everything was underground. Microwave ovens were always part of the equipment package and they weren't used to cook up a quick burger. They were invaluable as the fastest way to destroy evidence in case of a bust – look-outs with walkie-talkies gave you just enough time to blast the film from raw to well-done in a matter of seconds. Our thinking was that one re-shoot day was better than doing ten in the pen.'

Me: And what was the work like back then for the porn actors and actresses?

Him: Well, we've all heard the sad story of the midwest girl that follows her dreams of becoming a star in Hollywood, only to be swallowed by the seedy underworld of porn. For the most part this was true. Many girls grew tired of the 'casting couch', broken promises and not being able to pay their rent. The only acting these girls got to do was faking an orgasm while having to fuck some three-hundred-pound agent with a two-inch dick with performances that were doubtless worthy of an Oscar.

Is it any wonder these girls began to rationalise their involvement in porn? At least in porn they could practise the art of acting and get paid enough not only to pay their rent but even to support their families. Sure they had to fuck people, but was it any worse than what they were doing to try and get a small part in a movie? This scenario was advantageous for producers in the early days because it actually gave us access to people that really wanted to act even more than fuck. Back then, we truly wanted to make good movies. I'm not saying there aren't any good actors or actresses in the business now. What I am saying is that they are few and far between, and the emphasis of the majority of films is not on acting or creating a story, but on vile and disgusting acts to shock the viewer. I call it 'Jackass Porn', a term I picked up from Taylor Wane.

Me: So how do you find the situation today?
Him: Today, things are quite different. Porn can be produced by anyone with a $300 camera, a girlfriend willing to spread her legs, and a little Internet knowledge. Oddly enough, since it has become legal, it has also become more violent and dehumanising. Back in the day, we had a list of things you just don't

film and everyone stuck by that list. Today, other than bestiality and paedophilia, you would be hard-pressed to find a movie without everything on that list being exploited. It's become so violent – there have been two girls that recently suffered broken jaws. If you did these things to your wife at home you would be arrested for domestic violence and assault but somehow it seems to be perfectly OK on a porn set.

Me: I remember when I was filming with you, we started talking about the latest porn craze and you mentioned Donkey Punch videos – what's that all about?

Him: The Donkey Punch is very symbolic as to how porn has changed just as *Saw* is very symbolic as to how mainstream films have changed. They both represent how society has shifted. The Donkey Punch is a technique used during the filming of anal sex where the girl is being ridden doggy style and just as the guy comes in her ass he punches her in the back of the head hard enough to try and get her to pass out. Sexual? Erotic? To me, it's just a violent act carried out by people who hate women. It's a reflection of where society is headed rather than just a reflection of pornography.

Me: So is the future of porn one of violence and torture rather than... sex?

Him: Unfortunately I think the future of porn is already here. I believe it has now reached a point of no return where it is infiltrated with deviance rather than eroticism. Jackass Porn is satisfying to a new fan-base that demands far more degrading material than the norm. They are probably your typical guys that could never get a date – too nerdy, too fat or too

199

ugly – they sat back and watched the high school sports heroes nab the hot chicks. Now they hate women and feel good about watching them get abused. It's payback in some way. Currently it seems that the better looking the girl being degraded, the better they like it. Women are being tortured and brutalised on porn sets every day, and that's a tragic situation. Despite this, attitudes are becoming blasé, and all porn, no matter how degrading it is, is starting to become more accepted by audiences.

Me: Who do you think is to blame for this?
Him: Most people blame this escalation of violence and degradation on the abstract world of the porn industry rather than, say, people's parents or society in general. But it all starts with the child and the parents at home. When you have a President, the leader of the free world, make a ridiculous claim that getting a blowjob and leaving your semen on a woman's dress can be classified as not having sex and not being held accountable, you have a society in complete denial of a moral decay that goes well beyond the porn industry.

Me: So is there ever a temptation for someone like yourself to jump on the bandwagon and go more 'extreme' in order to stay ahead of the game?
Him: There is always temptation to survive, be it in life or in business. Am I tempted to compete with people that promote violence on women? No, never. No matter what you do in life, you have a responsibility to stop when your rights begin to cause harm to others.
The younger generation is looking for whores being treated like animals. These 'porn fans' are not the type of people I want to entertain. I always wanted to create beautifully photographed erotic scenarios that

200

entertained couples who wanted to spice up their sex lives in the confines of their home. Unfortunately, the overwhelming majority of porn films being made today are being made for degenerates, not couples. I do realise there are some risqué fetishes out there, but I think much like the way Alfred Hitchcock handled horror, with an element left to the imagination, these scenarios should be handled the same way. What's missing is the erotic nature that makes, say, a spanking, sexy rather than violent. So am I tempted to change the way I work to cater for a more hardcore audience? No. Not one bit. Trying to stay ahead in this game would only find me spiritually behind. When you've lost your spirit you've lost more than just your business – you've lost your will to live.

Speaking to Laurien again and hearing him refer to a more degenerate style of porn reminds me of a recent occasion when I was sitting round a poker table and someone's mobile phone went off. It turned out that a friend of his had sent him an Internet porn clip. He looked at it, started laughing and passed the phone around the table. I looked at it and on it was footage of a girl being screwed from behind by a horse. Even I, despite everything I have seen, was pretty shocked by this. Somehow, watching it, you are gripped by a terrible fascination, but you know in your heart this is so wrong. On so many levels. The reaction of most of those who saw it was the same as his: to laugh. But I wonder if they're really thinking straight – I hate to descend into cliché, but that girl is someone's daughter. I can't stop myself from thinking what kind of life that 'anonymous' girl has, who awakes the next morning, looks in the mirror and recalls the previous day. God only knows what she ends up thinking, but I suspect it wasn't part of the game-plan to have sex with a horse when she had the teenage hopes and dreams that we all share. This kind of material is typical of what Laurien calls Jackass Porn – something that is intended to shock rather than actually titillate an audience. At least I hope that's the case. But then again, who am I to judge whether something is right or wrong? Why should I condemn hardcore images just because they're not to my liking? I think there should be boundaries –I'm just not sure where those boundaries should be and I'm probably not the right man to set them.

I'd love to see more protection for porn actors and actresses – not least because I've met so many of them and have usually found them to be charming, open, honest and brave people. I no longer objectify them when I see them on screen; I see them as the real people that they are. And because of that I sympathise with them more than I ever used to and I'm concerned by current trends towards 'shock porn'. The more extreme porn becomes, the greater the demands on the mental and physical health of the actors and actresses. It's a vicious circle, because the more the audience is exposed to degenerate images, the bigger the shock value that will have to be created by film-makers in order to try and continue to impact upon the viewer.

So let's get back to the blame game. Who's at fault? I agree in part with Laurien: that a general breakdown in the values of society is at fault. So too are rogue producers. But more importantly, so too are we, the audience, and even the casual consumer, for helping to fuel the more extreme elements of pornographic film-making. Money talks: if we didn't buy or watch this stuff, it would disappear as quickly as it came on the scene. Luckily for me and my conscience, *Sin Cities* never really dealt with this material or these issues. It was more of a kick around, light-hearted kind of show – we often heard about the negative sides to the sex industry but it was rare that we ever came into contact with them. From what I saw, very few of those who worked in porn didn't appear to enjoy, at least in part, their job. For some, sure, it was because of the money and financial security it gave them, but others freely admitted to being turned on by having sex on camera, and the chance, however slim, of becoming a bona fide porn star. That's not to say they were all driven a by raging lust to work in porn. No, I think the vast majority of people in the industry are, bottom line, victims of circumstance... but I do think that a small minority also simply have far fewer sexual hang-ups than the rest of us.

Let's not also forget that where there is a female porn star there is usually a male one, and one who is invariably being paid around a third of what his female counterpart is receiving. Is he being exploited too? As porn becomes progressively more mainstream there is a growing number of female directors, and an increasing number of films that cater for the female consumer. Today, porn is not just a male arena – if people want to take issue with it, which they have every right to, then I think the objection should be a moral one rather than one based on gender.

Back in Budapest, after witnessing my first scene of double penetration, I interviewed the female star, asking her if she'd enjoyed the experience of a double helping of cock. She promptly told me that it had been 'amazing'. I voiced my own suspicions that she was possibly faking it – I implored her to be honest, and she insisted that it had been fantastic and she would do it all again in a second. Can't argue with that. Unfortunately for her, the two lads had shot their wads and were done for the day. I'm a natural cynic, but I have no hesitation in believing that she was telling me the truth.

I don't doubt that some women outside of porn also fantasise about things like DP, or perhaps having their own porn star experience. I think this, in part, explains the huge rise in homemade camcorder and mobile phone porn. It can't just be the boyfriend who wants to do these things, can it? No, it takes two to tango, and my hunch is that girls can be just as naughty when they're shown enough trust and respect. In my own sex life away from the cameras, I was once asked by an ex-girlfriend to re-create a scene from a porno where the star of the movie had been made airtight — namely a cock in the arse, vagina, and mouth. Being fairly open-minded, I decided to give her the next best thing, and hopped off to a sex shop to buy her a sparkling new dildo and butt plug. Cue one of the most amazing times I've ever had in the sack — every orifice was full, she loved it, and I, in turn, delighted in her joy — not to mention my own enjoyment at having my cock in her mouth to complete the treble.

Having heard all that, it may surprise you to hear that personally, I'm not really a huge fan of watching porn. Maybe that's because it's a bit of a comedown to see it on the small screen having witnessed so much of it in the flesh. I don't know, but it does usually seem... a bit disappointing. That's especially true of celebrity porn. Fair enough, it's true that celebrity sex tapes were not necessarily intended for broadcast, but when I see people like John Leslie and Abi Titmuss in action, I'm left astonished at how dull they are in the sack. Even if this two-hour pile of dross had been edited down into a brief highlights package, there would just be several moments of very boring, conventional copulation accompanied by some light moaning left for your viewing 'pleasure'. It's completely devoid of any rampant, no-holds-barred sex. To not put too fine a point on it, it's just a bit shit really. It amazes me that on the back of something so utterly uninspiring, Titmuss has gone on to become some kind of sex guru and semi-porno glamour girl. Honestly, we Brits must have really low standards if we hold up someone as crap in bed as Abi Titmuss as some kind of sexual goddess. I swear, I would have kicked her out within minutes.

And what about *One Night in Paris,* starring Paris Hilton and then-boyfriend, Rick Salomon? Well, I'm sorry, but if I was in the sack with someone as unresponsive as Paris then I'd be tempted to check her pulse and see if she still had a heartbeat. I just hoped, for her sake, she at least made him a decent breakfast.

I suppose, in a way, I'm encouraged when I see other people having such monotonous sex lives – especially celebrities, who you somehow expect to be wild and outrageous – because it makes me feel great about myself in bed. If you're having a crisis of confidence in the bedroom, just tune in to Paris or Abi for ten minutes or so and you'll soon consider yourself a magnificent sexual animal with some of the best moves in the business. I'm not saying I'm swinging off the chandeliers or anything, but fuck me, I'm a fucking sexual demon compared to most of the trash you see on those tapes. Only the Pamela Anderson/Tommy Lee sex tape has any real balls... and a sizeable pair at that.

After Budapest, I only ever saw double penetration one more time, and again, it was one of the most gob-smacking experiences of my life. Firstly, we arrived in LA to report on married couples who worked together in the adult industry and began by filming one of America's biggest porn stars – Taylor Wane – a British girl who had moved to LA and taken the world of porn by storm. Taylor and her director husband Laurien (who we've already heard from) successfully disproved the theory that true love couldn't exist in the sex industry. Taylor was a great girl, a bona fide porn star full of fun and adventure, boasting boobs that looked like balloons and an undiluted enthusiasm for making the pornos that Laurien would film and direct. I was surprised that such a close relationship could survive the rigours of working in the sex industry, but, through a mixture of professional detachment and trust, these two seemed, in a manner of speaking, to have it licked. 'Trust' may be an odd word to use when Taylor is getting screwed left, right and centre by other men, but they had such a close and sympathetic relationship that jealousy was simply not an issue for them. Off-camera, they were a sweet, charming couple and completely inseparable.

For me, all negative stereotypes of the adult industry were blown away during my time with Taylor and Laurien, and I was genuinely gutted when our schedule meant we had to leave 'the house that porn built', as Taylor proudly described her million-dollar mansion. But it wasn't all bad – just around the corner was a porn shoot that would soon put a smile back on my face and introduce me once more to the visual feast of double penetration.

Larry and Debbie Schwarz were a married couple also living and working in LA. When we arrived to film them, they gave us a very brief history of their relationship, which I shall now share with you, my friend, in order to help put you in the picture.

Larry, who was in his sixties, and Debbie, who was turning fifty that day, had been married for over twenty-five years. They had one daughter, Stephany, who had earlier moved to California to pursue a career working in the sex industry, and starred as a porn actress in some 200 hard core films, under the spectacular stage name

Jewel De'Nyle. Debbie, who had proclaimed herself the 'proud parent of a porn star', had now decided to follow in her daughter's footsteps to LA and into the sex industry, performing as a novelty middle-aged porn actress under the less remarkable moniker De'Bella.

Under this name, she had now racked up a considerable number of porn titles herself, including the aptly named *Momma Knows Best, Lesbian Mature Women* and *Muff Munchin' Milfs*. Stop laughing, I have a copy of *Muff Munchin' Milfs* and it's a belter. Although her daughter had since stopped working as a porn actress and strongly disapproved of her mother's new career to the point of dismissing her as 'a crack whore', husband Larry was a big fan of De'Bella's work. When I spoke to him, he explained that he loved her unconditionally and was determined to support her, whatever she decided to do. He also claimed that due to his age he was no longer able to fully satisfy his wife in the bedroom. Working as a porn actress was, he believed, now providing her with all her necessary sexual satisfaction as well as semi-decent earning potential. Jealousy and possessiveness, he told me, had long since disappeared from their relationship.

On the day of filming, it was De'Bella's 50th birthday and she was celebrating the occasion by taking part in a new porn flick, *Nifty Fifties & Anal*, where she claimed she would be doing anal for the first time with not one, not two, but three male porn actors. I was suspicious that this might not be her first delve into fudge-nudging: surely a middle-aged woman now immersed in the porn industry had done anal? As De'Bella was having her make-up done in preparation for the upcoming shoot, I asked her if this was really the case. In a flash, I was faced with the slightly disturbing sight of De'Bella reaching beneath her underwear to pull out a sizeable butt plug from her back passage.

'It really is my first time – see. I'm loosening up in preparation!'

'Oh my god,' I stammered. 'Has that just come out of your bottom?!'

'Sure,' she replied. 'I thought it was a good idea after speaking to the boys – they said they were gonna tear me a new one.'

With that, De'Bella proceeded to deep-throat her freshly extracted butt plug just inches away from my face. De'Bella, it was clear, was an entertainer, determined to put on a good show. As I sat looking at her, I was struck by such downright naughtiness coming from someone old enough to be my own mother. De'Bella, it's safe to say, wasn't the most classically attractive girl, but what she did have, and what is perhaps the most valuable attribute for any aspiring porn starlet, was an aura of total sluttishness. My suspicion, after our initial meeting, was that De'Bella would be a revelation on set.

The filming location was a huge house on a private estate, owned by an Italian director and built entirely on the proceeds of a successful career in pornography. After musing over the possibility of changing careers and diving headfirst into a world of porn and ready cash, I had another chat with De'Bella about her being a married woman. I suggested to her that maybe a move into porn wasn't the ideal way to sustain a healthy relationship with her husband. De'Bella, however, was adamant that she had the full support of Larry. For her it was very simple.

'He wants me to be happy and doing this makes me happy. And if I'm happy, then he's happy.'

Although I could relate to that, I wondered what Larry was getting out of the deal while his missus enjoyed being shagged senseless. If I was to get married then the thought of my wife banging other men on a porn set would horrify me. But Larry found himself turned on by his wife's enjoyment, and if his motivations were as selfless as he made out, then that's nothing to be sniffed at. I think it takes a strong man to release himself from claiming his wife's body as his own possession and allow her to share it with other people, no strings attached. Well, either a strong man or a very weak man who allows his wife to walk all over him. De'Bella then revealed that although her man was supportive of her new career, he had yet to actually witness her in action. Today, however, that was all about to change – Larry was going to see her on set for the very first time. It's hard not to feel some sense that surely De'Bella and Larry's relationship was a dysfunctional one. This was far from normal, wasn't it? But then again, who am I to say that my lifestyle and my values are right and that Larry and De'Bella's were in any way wrong? My view at the time was that they had gone into this with their eyes wide open and had struck upon the fact that this was something De'Bella was good at, wanted, was perhaps lacking in her personal life and was being paid good money to do.

As things were to turn out, De'Bella was going to earn every penny of her fee. When I spoke to the three strapping lads who would be nailing De'Bella ragged and treating her to an anal onslaught, I almost winced. All three boasted huge members – none of them was below the eight-inch mark, and all of them packed some serious girth. I was starting to get seriously fearful for the health and safety of De'Bella's ring-piece. I was also a little surprised to see that the boys were all in their early twenties and quite happy to be shagging a middle-aged woman, slightly rough around the edges, with her husband in attendance.

Ashley: But would you manage to keep a stiffy even if

you didn't fancy her?

The boys: No problem, we're professionals.

Me: Did you know that De'Bella claimed never to have done anal before?

Them: We heard that. She'll enjoy it.

Me: I notice you're all masturbating while talking to me now. Is this a gay thing?

Them: No, we have to get stiff for filming.

Me: Phew.

De'Bella, it has to be said, was by now looking visibly excited, and after an initial photo-shoot downstairs she walked into the bedroom where the boys were sat, and without so much as a word of introduction, sat down and began sucking one of them off. Now, bearing in mind the cameras were not even rolling at this point, I instantly knew De'Bella was going to be treating us to a particularly memorable afternoon. Surely though, despite her enthusiastic start, these three big boys were going to prove more than a handful for the birthday girl? And what about her arse, for fuck's sake?!

As filming kicked off, I was struck by De'Bella's unabashed enthusiasm for the job in hand, regardless of the fact that her husband was sat just yards away on a sofa, watching the action unfurl. Said action involved a variety of full-on hardcore porn: first, De'Bella was fucked by all three men in all manner of positions, then she was screwed by one lad while sucking off another, after that she was taken up the wrong 'un by one boy while another fucked her mouth... the list of combinations goes on. They must have been filming for well over an hour and there was no let up. De'Bella was getting well and truly rogered, and appeared to be relishing every second of it.

She was extremely vocal, crying out for more, begging her cohorts not to stop, and continually screaming out that she was on the verge of orgasm.

'Don't stop! Fuck me harder! Oh my God, I'm gonna cum! Fuck me, oh yeah, oh yeah, that's it! Keep going – fuck me, oh God yes, fuck me!'

Gee whizz! As the cries grew ever louder, I sought out a seat next to Larry, who was sat impassively watching his wife in the throes of apparent sexual rapture.

'Hey Larry, how's it hanging?'

'Pretty good.'

'De'Bella seems to be enjoying herself.'

A prolonged conversation with Larry was difficult bearing in mind we could hardly hear ourselves think over and above the screams of ecstasy from De'Bella as she revelled in the joys of getting triple-teamed. Then, we heard a sudden break in filming... De'Bella, it appeared, had suffered a slight injury. Avoiding the sweating male bodies and protruding penises, I went over to her to check she was OK.

'I just spotted some blood,' she said. 'I think it's from my ass-hole.'

She grabbed some tissue and started wiping. 'Yeah, my ass is bleeding.'

I turned to camera and immediately informed our viewers that 'two orifices have now become one'.

This, I confess, this was a facetious and rather trite comment, especially bearing in mind that De'Bella was in danger of suffering some kind of anal fall-out, a prospect which didn't bear thinking about. But despite her injury, De'Bella resolved to carry on. The boys, too, were in no mood to back off – one of them, who went by the name of John Strong, was proving to be an awesome performer. In what must have stretched to well over two hours of filming, he kept pumping away virtually non-stop. His side-kicks were no slouches either, and when they weren't screwing on camera they were stood on the sidelines, cocks in hand, masturbating away in order to maintain their hard-ons.

The next scene, in fact, has now taken its place at the top of my pantheon of Most Amazing Porn Moments. De'Bella braced herself for something I had never before seen on camera – double penetration from two guys in standing position. De'Bella was held in what I like to call 'the monkey position' by one of the lads (probably John Strong) – in other words, she was wrapped around his chest while he fucked her from the front. As he was doing so, one of the other boys approached De'Bella from behind, held his cock in his hand and then guided it into her backside. Holy fuck!! De'Bella then rocked herself up and down so that both co-stars were moving in and out of her at the same time – extraordinary. Restraining myself from breaking into loud applause, I stood with my mouth wide open. Truly, this was an incredible display of unadulterated hardcore sex. Seeing it in real life was astonishing. What's more, the total pleasure that emanated from De'Bella was actually quite titillating – it's rare that I feel any stirrings on the set of a porno, but De'Bella's enthusiasm was so infectious that I was moved to get my mobile phone out and capture a few seconds of footage for posterity's sake. Sadly that particular phone has since been stolen – I only hope the footage wasn't wasted on the fucker who nicked it.

I didn't fancy De'Bella in the slightest, neither would I have had any wish to join in and make it a foursome if the opportunity arose; but what I do find sexy about women is what De'Bella had – a tangible love of sex. And believe me, if anyone wanted to claim that De'Bella hadn't enjoyed herself that afternoon, they would have been laughed off set. As indeed I probably would have

212

been if I had made any moves to join in the action. Between them, the male actors had provided De'Bella with some 24 inches of cock... she would scarcely have noticed my presence had I joined in and made it 27.

As De'Bella's double penetration scene began to run out of steam, the director signalled that it was time to wrap things up. As many of you will no doubt know, the vast majority of current pornos tend to finish with the male performers climaxing over the face of the female actress. De'Bella, however, voiced her own preference: 'One in the ass, one in the pussy and one in my mouth,' she called. To my surprise, she was overruled. The director, being a purist, wanted to go for the traditional finish of all three lads jacking off over De'Bella's face. De'Bella's disappointment didn't last long as she grabbed and sucked away at all three cocks until finally they were ready to cum. Bish, bash, bosh: De'Bella was soon a mass of runny semen-stained make-up and cheap perfume. And with filming done and dusted, Larry approached his newly baptised wife. Surely he wasn't going to give her a well done kiss? Please God, no! Instead, to my relief, Larry handed De'Bella a towel.

'Well done, darling. I think you'd better have a shower.'

Yeah, that should do the trick. I was left wondering what they spoke about over dinner that night.

'Can you pass the salt please, dear. Oh, and how's the arse? Still a bit tender?'

chapter 17
vixen and lara

There were only a couple of other occasions when I met female characters who came close to having De'Bella's passion for sex. One such enthusiast went by the appropriately racy name of Vixen. Rather than making top shelf videos however, Vixen spread her legs all over the Internet by making live sex broadcasts from her downstairs living room. I say legs, but I should really qualify that – Vixen, you see, had very little legs. She can't have been more than four foot four inches tall. But within that diminutive figure lay an insatiable appetite for sex.

She and her husband would set up Internet broadcasts of orgies from their house in Philadelphia, which were imaginatively called 'Philly Fucking Parties'. Hordes of horny men of all shapes and sizes would gather around as Vixen and her female friends started by cuddling on a platform of mattresses. Then the guys were invited to join them until the mass of participants developed into a sea of writhing, naked bodies.

When I headed downstairs after doing some interviews, I was faced with the sight of Vixen being spit-roasted. From behind she was being screwed by an enormous black guy, while at her front end another lad was enjoying what I suspect was a supremely well-practised blowjob. At least ten eager male participants formed an orderly queue behind, each awaiting their turn, all of them cocks in hand, preparing to deliver their meat feasts to Vixen.

It's quite difficult to describe what it's like to be in a situation like that, surrounded by naked men, all wanking away, while various other people are having full-on sex. Part of me finds it exciting, another part of me thinks it's a bit sordid and desperate… but on the whole, as long as everyone present is consensual and happy doing what they're doing, then I try not to make any judgement one way or the other. One of the main surprises when you go to an orgy like the one Vixen was hosting, is that even though it seems like a free-for-all, there are very strict rules of behaviour and etiquette. These were set out by Vixen at the beginning of the evening when she explained that first and foremost: 'no means no'. Secondly, the men were not allowed to initiate sexual activity but had to wait until they were invited to take part in sex. I guess this was a rule that most of these guys were happy to adhere to, especially since it seemed only a matter of time before they would get the invite. Of the many sex parties I've been to, not once did I ever see a man move out of line for fear that he would suffer the indignity of being thrown out. In fact, the only person I have seen being shown the door at a swingers' party was my good self, after a girl at a party in Vancouver made a move on me and I complained that her tits were too small. This was by no means untruthful, but it turned out that she had taken offence, complained to the host of the evening and I was politely asked to leave. I had broken the unspoken code of conduct: show respect to everyone at all times. Darn it, I guess I wasn't really cut out to be a swinger.

At Vixen's place, I was in no mood to join in the sexual frolics. Well, I say that, but there was always a part of me that would have loved to dive in and shag away for England. But again, I hesitate in saying that, because the truth is I'm more of a one-on-one, preferably without an audience, kind of guy. There is, after all, the issue of having sloppy seconds, or even sloppy thirds, fourths or fifths. The idea of stirring someone else's porridge just doesn't do it for me. I mean, when you know you're just another case study in a long line of men, it can't make you feel all that special can it?

Vixen, however, had no such scruples. But there was a tragic underside to her story. She was suffering from a serious debilitating illness – I forget exactly what – and her life-expectancy had diminished considerably. She probably wouldn't make it much beyond her forties and was eager to make the most of what little time she had left by treating herself to as much sexual pleasure as she could possibly find. The sad truth, therefore, was that the Philly Fucking Parties were very far from being the joyous, extravagant invention of a carefree and liberated mind, but were instead one woman's means of making the best of a bad lot. Sex was her way of saying 'I exist,' something she screamed from the rooftops, or more specifically, from the Internet. Sex was essential to her sense of self-worth, an integral part of her make-up, and hosting sex parties was the best use of the time she had left.

Strangely, despite the fact that I've ended up working in such a highly charged sexual environment, my own sex drive – at least compared to someone like Vixen's – is probably fairly average. Usually with me it goes in waves; sometimes I feel rampant and at other times completely disinterested. This, annoyingly, has often affected my personal life where a period of disinterest in sex has caused several tearful break-ups. Then again, if the truth be told, I think some of my relationships have ended not through my own lack of interest in sex, but due to feeling jaded with the monotony of just having sex with the same person. When you're in the first throes of a love affair, romance lures you into thinking you'll never stop fancying your new partner. And then it slowly creeps up on you – the initial rush of fancying the pants off your girlfriend has gone, and when you go to the pub together you start looking at other women. Then, you may pass someone on the street who you think is hotter than your missus and you start to wonder what it would be like to have sex with someone else. I hate it when this happens, because then I know I'm doomed.

You find yourselves in bed together and you're thinking 'Hmm, I miss not being able to go out and just try it on with anyone.' And before you know it, despite the fact that you loathe yourself for it, you end up preferring the thought of having sex with someone you don't even know rather than the person you actually love. But that, I guess, is a massive biological fault line running through my body (and, I assume, that of many other men). And it makes me despair.

Which I suppose brings me to people like Vixen and other swingers like her. Because they don't mind their partners seeing other people, they can still maintain a happy relationship while satisfying their desire to sleep around. For swingers, sex doesn't have to be exclusive, and that's something they often claim helps them appreciate their partner and enhances their own sex lives together. Maybe the answer is to be found in having an open relationship – but some people, me included, find that while on paper that sounds fine, in practice it can be complicated and difficult. Our friend Vixen obviously had no problems with this whatsoever. Her husband too, despite suffering no illness himself, also seemed pretty keen not to waste any time in racking up as many notches on his bedpost as possible. At one stage in the evening he boasted to me that he'd had no less than nine blowjobs that night. I had no reason to disbelieve him – I had, after all, seen him get sucked off by at least three different girls at various stages throughout the evening. After we finished filming I was just about to leave when Vixen called out to me, 'You can't leave now; I haven't sucked your cock yet. Come back here! I'll suck your cock!' Vixen's sweet words echoed in the distance as I left her in the comforting arms of her husband who, in my absence, I'm sure was looking forward to the imminent tenth blowjob.

I was to receive a similarly generous offer of sexual favours when, some years later, I visited an English porn actress in the suburbs of Melbourne, Australia. Like De'Bella and Vixen, Lara James immediately struck me with her unabashed enthusiasm for sex and provided me with one of my best-ever days on the *Sin Cities* road.

Lara, who it turned out was originally from Sheffield in Yorkshire, was due to be filming a gang bang video with five Aussie blokes who looked like they were all on day release from prison. This, however, didn't put Lara off one little bit. Although she was fairly new to the porn scene, Lara was eager to get straight down to fucking – a sure sign of impending greatness in the world of porn. When we turned up for the shoot, Lara was keen to get cracking and show off her full repertoire of bedroom gymnastics. Insisting on a quick chat before the main event, I led her outside for a quick get-to-know-you session. There, she surprised me by revealing how she'd ended up in the industry.

'I got into doing porn because I had a car accident. I was a nurse and doing some part-time modelling. After the accident I couldn't nurse anymore because I broke my hand so I started doing porn to make a little bit more money. And I love doing it. I'm the same person I was before – a caring woman that has looked after people all her life. I love sex and I love meeting people. If it's done safely and responsibly, then it's fine.'

'Back when you were twenty though,' I asked, 'did you think you'd end up doing porn and – bearing in mind that's what you do – do you have any regrets?'

'I have no regrets in my life, what I've done in the past is what has made me what I am today. I love me. I am a wonderful, loving, kind person that anyone would be proud to associate with,' she said.

Lara then looked at me, laughed, and revealed that she'd got me mixed up with British TV chef Ainsley Harriot. Having expected a great big smiley black geezer, poor Lara had instead ended up with me! How on earth she thought that Ainsley had moved on from afternoon cookery shows on the BBC to covering hardcore porn on cable was utterly beyond me, but there you go. Despite her understandable disappointment, we continued our conversation and Lara went on to reveal that despite being married with two children, she was not just building a career as a budding porn star but had also branched out into working as an escort.

Ashley: OK, so let's get this straight: you do porn and you're an escort, but you're married with children?
Lara: Yes, that's right, darling.

Me: Why isn't your husband here now?

Her: He works nights. And that last answer shows the difference in mind-set between the people who work in porn and those who do not. It's not like her husband wouldn't show up because he was disgusted at the thought of his wife getting laid by half a dozen Aussies. No, he worked nights and couldn't get a sick note in time to come along and watch. Amazing.

Me: Your escort work... what's that like?

Her: Escorting is a service. It's lovely to make people happy. Some men are lonely. Some have had permission to go to an escort by their wives, fearing they would find another girlfriend if not. Some women don't enjoy sex at certain times in their lives or find it painful. Again, if you are professional and treat everyone with respect you find you get it back ten-fold.

Me: But how does escorting and porn affect how you view men?

Her: It doesn't affect me one bit. I love one man, my partner. It is my job to do the other. It is enjoyable but it's not a mental thing so I don't get the two confused at all. Men just want to fuck me and try things out.

Looking at Lara, I was starting to understand why. Although she was, shall we say, a mature lady, she scrubbed up pretty well. When I asked her how much she charged for her escorting services, Lara insisted she would give me a freebie. As I pondered whether or not to take her up on that offer, Lara was ushered on set, where her imminent sex partners were awaiting her arrival. Within a matter of seconds she was lying naked on a makeshift bed, head bobbing back and forth as she pleasured one chap, while another prepared himself for entry. I chatted to one of the remaining guys who had yet to join in the action. He was a geeky-looking lad in his twenties with long black hair pulled back into a pony tail. He looked like someone who hadn't left his bedroom for months due to an addiction to playing computer games – your typical *Dungeons and Dragons* nerd. I asked him why he'd come along today, and he told me straight away that it was because he wanted to lick Lara's arsehole. I was caught ever so slightly off guard.

'You what?'

'Yeah, I love rimming mate. It's my favourite thing.'

Now here was a man who knew what he wanted. Forget what I said about *Dungeons and Dragons*, it seemed this lad did indeed have some specialised interests in life, although they plainly had nothing to do with board games and everything to do with the female ring-piece. As he moved onto the bed he knelt down and proceeded to rim the lucky Lara until her backside was as clean as a whistle. The other lads weren't exactly hanging around either. One of them, Mick, entered Lara and pounded away while the others enjoyed blowjobs, hand-jobs, tit-jobs, courtesy of the lovely Lara. Indeed, as she was moved from one position to another she proclaimed her wish to be used and abused as they saw fit.

'Ooh yeah,' she said. 'That's it, treat me like a rubber doll, I love it.'

With that, Mick withdrew his penis and came all over Lara's stomach. It must have been the rubber doll comment that sent him over the edge. As the semen was perfunctorily wiped away, another lad stepped in to take Mick's place and the dream of seeing Lara in action as my own personal escort began to fade gently away. Then, seeing me standing there with my jaw resting quietly on the floor, Lara turned to me, spots of semen now clearly visible on her face, 'Well, don't just stand there love!

Come and get stuck in!'

'Thanks Lara, that's a very sweet offer,' I replied. 'But no thanks.'

With that, I said my fond farewells, with Lara and the boys still hard at it. No handshakes, no kisses on the cheek, thanks. I was off. As I cast a final glance behind me, I was left with an all-too-vivid memory: Lara, surrounded by a sea of sweaty Aussies, an English mother-of-two now bathed in bodily fluids and crying out for more. What a day and what a woman. Makes me proud to be British.

chapter 18
head fuck

I never looked forward to going to Germany on my travels: as a country it just seems a bit corporate. Also, let's ditch political correctness here, German people don't really float my boat – they just seem to try a bit too hard. Unfortunately for Anglo-German relations, the next filming assignment was not going to change my opinion.

If I thought my meeting with Lara had been messy, well, let's just say that was a mere walk in the park compared to what I would face in Deutschland. That afternoon, we arrived at a beat-up old nightclub where a local porn producer had arranged a bukkake shoot. I've already spoken about how the vast majority of niff-flicks end up with a facial cum shot. Bukkake, which originated in Japan as the punishment for an unfaithful wife, is a more extreme version of that, involving multiple male partners. In this case, it would involve seventy men shooting their individual loads over a single woman. Yep, let that register for a few seconds: seventy men, one girl.

It promised to get very messy indeed.

Bukkake is, I think, still one sex act that people tend to tiptoe around – even I feel a bit wary of talking about it here because I'm slightly fearful of aligning myself with something so notorious. There's no doubt however, and a simple search on the Internet confirms this, that it boasts a huge following. Thousands of web sites dedicate themselves to showing pictures and videos of female faces being drenched in cum. My opinion is, like most men (I assume), that part of me finds it disgusting and part of me finds it arousing and horny. I think perhaps it's titillating because it's one of the few things that veer into the realms of taboo. In modern society, we have all become so numb and desensitised to sex and sexual imagery that it takes an increasingly extreme image to provoke revulsion – and bukkake is one of the few things that still does that. I sometimes can't help but find slutty imagery attractive. For me, there's nothing better than the thought that a girl loves sex, and an image of her with cum all over herself, however deluded or false an impression it may be, suggests an enthusiasm for sex. On the other hand, I also find it a bit grim because the image of so much semen all over the face of a girl... well, it's just a bit fucking wrong isn't it? If I was to switch sexes for a second and put myself in the girl's position, I would feel used, abused, degraded... a victim rather than an equal participant.

Despite these contradictions (yeah, I know, sex is confusing and complex) I remain a big fan of coming on a girl's face and I'm not ashamed to admit that. I understand some people may think it's an insulting sexual act but in my own private life I never did it as a means of debasing my partner. At least I was never conscious of that being my motivation – if any misogynistic motivation exists in my unconscious psyche, well then so be it, but

I'm not aware of it. For me, it's the taboo nature of the act that makes it thrilling and attractive. Also, on a more basic level, if you're having sex for fun rather than procreation, it makes sense to cum somewhere other than the muff. The face is an extremely attractive part of a woman and to shoot your load there can sometimes be part of a natural progression in the bedroom. Likewise, I can highly recommend the tits and arse as equally viable alternatives. Perhaps surprisingly, of the girls I've slept with and with whom I was comfortable enough to broach the subject of an orgasm to the face, I would say around 80 percent of them were keen for me to do it – and by that I'm not saying they reluctantly lay back and went, 'Oh God, alright then, if you must.' It was: 'Go for it, Ash!' Women, I think, are sometimes not so different from men – if you get on and like each other, then you usually want to try and experiment with different things and a facial cum shot is just one of those things.

One time, I ended up in bed for the first time with a girl who wasn't on the pill and I was out of rubbers. When I was nearing the point of no return, I asked, 'Where do you want me to cum – we've got three options: stomach, tits or face?'

'Face, please,' came the instant reply.

'Right answer.'

That particular girl became one of the few loves of my life and, let me make this clear, I never thought any worse of her for wanting me to come on her face. Instead, it was one of the many things I adored about her.

But enough about me and my sordid little life; let's instead concentrate on how awful the Germans are. And that day, they were seriously rank. I arrived at this nightclub for the bukkake shoot and there were already a fair few blokes milling around waiting for the action to start. Things were set to warm up with a sex show starring a young female and some local bloke who looked to be the German equivalent of Ron Jeremy – minus the charm. The girl, called Martina, had driven to Berlin from her home in Prague. She was a typical-looking Eastern European porn starlet – in other words, she was fucking gorgeous – aged about twenty with long blonde hair, a very pretty face and perfectly proportioned body. Why would a girl like that want to do something like this? That is, of course, a question I have asked myself many times, and I always make an effort to stop myself, because it suggests that she has made a bad choice. But it is not necessarily a bad choice – it's just her choice. In fact, I hate making negative judgments on people in the sex industry when you could just as easily argue that a girl who hangs out in China White's hoping to snag a millionaire footballer is just one small step away from prostitution.

I met Martina before she started her shift – and for her I imagine that's all it was, just another day at the office – and she looked fantastic. Her male co-star, as I've said, looked horrible – hairy, middle-aged, overweight and sweaty. This, I assume was another ploy by the director to make his finished porn film more accessible to viewers – the idea being that, 'Hey, if this guy can fuck this girl, then I could too.' Or at least imagine yourself doing so.

When they were done, it was time for a few minutes' break before the bukkake shoot. Well, it wasn't really a break as such, it was now time for the rest of the men in the room, all 70 of them, to limber up, harness an erection, and prepare for their few moments in the limelight. Specifically to this end, two fluffers had been provided. I had never before seen fluffers in action. Renowned as being the lowest rung on the ladder in the adult industry, the fluffer is a girl employed for the sole purpose of giving the male stars a hard-on. In this instance there were two girls sat on stools at the back of the nightclub, servicing any penis that was thrust towards them – and at this shoot, that was a lot of cock. Stood in scarcely concealed astonishment, I struck up conversation with the chap standing next to me, who it turned out was the boyfriend of one of the fluffers. I mean, *what the fuck?* Can you imagine being present when your supposed-girlfriend is sucking serious amounts of dick? This, my friends, redefined the term 'open relationship'. Hordes of horny Germans were jostling for position around the fluffers, and for some time thereafter I felt a unique feeling welling up inside me – a feeling that I was slightly ashamed to be a man. By being a man I felt, by proxy, like I was somehow associated with these grubby characters, all milling around with their cocks out, wanking away, eagerly awaiting their chance to spill their seed over a girl they couldn't hope to have a chance with outside of the day's activities.

But rubbing shoulders with masturbating men wasn't exactly a new experience for me, so why was this any different? I think what distinguished this occasion from other porn shoots I had attended was the complete lack of any humour, dignity or camaraderie. In short, it was bereft of any sense of fun or entertainment. I'm not saying that every other porn shoot was a constant stream of jokes and laughter, but there was usually a lightness of touch, a ray of hope that shone through the haze of sleaze. Here, there were no such saving graces. Instead, I had the unsettling feeling that I was bearing witness to the self-serving physical satisfaction of 70 anonymous men who had answered some dodgy advert in the back pages of a tawdry German porn mag. Which they probably had.

Soon enough they were to get what they'd been waiting for, as everyone was asked to line up in two equal queues to the left and right of Martina, who was on her knees in the centre of the room. One by one, cock in hand, they would approach her – one from the left, then one from the right – to deliver their own individual dollops of semen. By the time ten or fifteen of them had done this, Martina was in a right old state. Although she didn't seem in the least bit bothered, her face was literally covered in cum. I don't really want to go into details of how she looked after all 70 had been and done their bit, but you can guess that it was more than enough to inspire a severe bout of nausea. For the participants, though, it just seemed like a very routine afternoon. However, none of them seemed to enjoy the process – it was all about self and nothing else. Nearly half of them appeared so starved of sexual activity that within minutes of ejaculation number one, they joined the back of the queue for a second bite at the cherry. On a physical level at least, they must have gained some pleasure from it, but it still seemed a very joyless occasion. To make matters worse, the director came up to me as things were coming to a close and, with a sleazy grin plastered across his face, asked me if I wanted to have a go. The words 'fuck right off' came immediately to mind. Weakly, I said 'no thanks', and concerned myself with thinking how the fuck Martina was going to be able to come to terms with what she had just done, or, perhaps more accurately, had had done to her.

It has to be said that at no time did she appear to be in any distress, but I couldn't help but speculate on what would be going through her mind as she drove back to Prague that night. I wonder if I'm being narrow-minded by feeling sorry for her – she did what she did for reasons that are beyond me. It can't surely be just about the pay cheque can it? Or am I being naïve? Perhaps she was just trying to make ends meet... but millions of other Eastern European girls do that without turning to porn. Perhaps she was greedy, ambitious; perhaps she had a soft spot for man-juice. Seriously though, was she a victim here? There's no disputing the fact that she had been utterly objectified in the minds of all the men gathered there that day. Still, at least she had her fee to console herself with – the men who had spilled their seed on her had nothing but an empty ball sack to attest to their involvement that day. As the film wrapped, Martina got up, semen streaming down her, wiped herself off with a towel, and disappeared into the bathroom. Never was a shower more needed and so well deserved.

In my opinion, behaviour that is commonly perceived as sleazy or sordid can always be forgiven if it's done in the right spirit. Take, for instance, my meeting with Extreme Elvis, a twenty-stone Elvis impersonator complete with mutton chop sideburns and white sequin suit. His act included stripping off naked, rubbing himself up against members of his audience, pissing on them, and taking a shit on stage. Extreme is a notorious figure. He has been banned from a number of venues across the States, including LA's world-famous Viper Room – where he was escorted from the venue by police after urinating on his contract, a contract which stipulated that there was to be no male nudity on stage.

When we met up, I was instantly taken by him. To me, he seemed like a very nice lad, doing his best to bring a bit of joy to people's lives. Well, I guess 'joy' may not be quite the right word – let's just say fun and excitement, and perhaps a healthy touch of revulsion. His audience demanded the outrageous and he was there to deliver. And trust me, he certainly delivered when the *Sin Cities* team paid him a visit one night in San Francisco.

Extreme Elvis and his band began by delivering a quality performance of some well-known Elvis Presley covers, all sung with expert aplomb, and received with rapturous applause. A baying mob of people soon reached fever pitch as Elvis began to strip. He then plunged off stage, fully naked — belly flowing, man-boobs bouncing and penis flailing as he belted out his songs in the midst of an increasingly hysterical crowd. Unfortunately for me, it appeared I was his chosen victim that night, and as he approached me, I sensed that things were about to go seriously awry. Elvis jumped on top of me; I collapsed under his weight, fell to the floor and was faced with the monstrous sight of a very large male, clad only in Elvis shades, with one hand on his microphone, the other on his penis. As he continued belting out the chorus to *Love Me Tender*, a spray of urine erupted from his cock and landed right on my face. Holy fuck! Now, understand this, normally I would have been tempted to lamp anyone who attempted such a stunt, but in this instance I couldn't stop laughing. More piss kept drizzling down, soaking my head and shoulders, until I managed to squirm away from under him, and thankfully, he was left to focus his spray elsewhere.

Disgusting? I thought Extreme Elvis was brilliant. In fact, I have since earmarked him as someone I want to play at my wedding should I ever get married. Well, maybe not the wedding, but definitely the stag night. While I would strongly object to anyone pissing in my face, even if I really liked them, in this case I found it welcome light relief. And that for me was the difference between the bukkake filming session and my meeting with Extreme Elvis: if it's entertainment, I can bring myself to embrace it. If it isn't, I can't. Extreme Elvis may not be to everyone's taste, and I can understand why, but

I thought he was fucking marvellous.

I guess I am pretty much of the school of thought that you shouldn't knock it till you've tried it. I say that because there have been many times when my own prejudices have been totally misplaced. This is why I am always keen to adopt a more immersive style of reporting. In the case of adult babies and infantilism, it would have been very easy to stand back and laugh and say how ridiculous it looks and dismiss it as some sort of bizarre and outlandish fancy dress fetish. But if you really get stuck into the actual process and keep an open mind you learn to understand how it provides immense joy and satisfaction (not necessarily sexual) to its participants.

Another example of this is when I went to visit Candy Godiva, a massively overweight woman who lived in New Orleans. There, I was to find my prejudices very swiftly swept away. On a really superficial level, I thought fat people were unattractive and ugly. Maybe they were just lazy – why don't they go on a diet, do some exercise, improve themselves and look better? So when I heard we were going to be filming Miss Godiva somewhere in the city suburbs, I went along reluctantly, assuming this was just going to be a bit of a freak show, and not something that I would be able to sink my teeth into and enjoy.

Now, there are fat people and there are very fat people. Candy was very very, very fat. In fact, let's not mince our words here, Candy was fucking enormous. Although she was only about five foot tall, Candy was nearly four foot wide and heavier than Extreme Elvis. Great swathes of flesh literally tumbled down from around her frame. I had never seen anything like it before in my life. This, to be sure, was one big bird: when she lifted her arms up, there were huge folds of hidden flab making their first forays from beneath her armpits for what must have been weeks. It was not a pretty sight, for beneath each fold I could make out sores from areas of skin that hadn't seen the light of day for far too long. Despite all this, Candy said she was more than happy with the way she looked, and so too was her boyfriend and photographer, Thomas. I had heard about people called 'feeders' who actively encouraged their girlfriends to put on weight, feeding them to the point where they become extremely unhealthy and bed-ridden. Thomas, however, insisted he was not a feeder – he just liked big women. Given the option of a catwalk model and Candy, Thomas would go for Candy every time.

After my initial discomfort at seeing her, I was soon put at ease by Candy's charm – and even physically, I started to quite like her. The more I spoke and got to know her, the more I found myself drawn into admiring her brazen attitude and yes, even her body. Rather than being turned off by it, I was starting to empathise with Thomas and began to think of Candy as one big play-ground. When chatting to her, I noticed a very sexy glint in her eye. This was a woman who revelled in her size and was keen to show herself off to me. And for me, that's the secret of sex appeal: show me a conventionally sexy and gorgeous female who hates herself and I'll run a mile. Give me a plain, non-descript someone who believes she's the sexiest thing on the planet and I'm hooked.

In the past, I've had a couple of flings with girls who, though I considered them to be amongst the sexiest mother-fuckers to walk the planet, successfully managed to persuade me that they were no longer attractive – purely because that was the low self-opinion they had of themselves. One ex-girlfriend I remember seeing for the first time and thinking, in the simplest possible way, 'Christ, I want that.' Before too long, however, it was obvious she had some major issues with her body image, yet for me, she was perfect and I wouldn't have changed a thing about her. Soon enough though, after just a few weeks together, she began to insist that I found other women more attractive than her (I didn't), a suspicion that soon mutated into being convinced I was having sex with other girls (I wasn't). As arguments escalated, her anticipation that I no longer found her attractive began to gain ground in reality – the more she insisted to herself and to me that she was not the beautiful creature I thought she was, the more I found it hard to disagree. When one of the things you find most attractive in someone is their sense of sexual self-worth, then it's pretty hard to start disagreeing with them when they insist they are not sexy. I mean, the last thing a man wants to hear from the girl he is shagging is the same girl telling him how worthless and unattractive she is. That just makes you think, 'Well, blimey, if that's your opinion, what the fuck am I doing with you?'

Even worse are constant and false accusations of infidelity, which leave a man just wanting to go out and have a string of affairs in order to justify the very same accusations... at least that way, in my case, I could have been blamed for something I'd actually done. It was a no-win situation: the more she insisted on her unattractiveness, the more inclined I was to believe her. And that of course, in turn, reinforced her lack of self-worth. Before too long, I lost any real desire to have sex with her. If she didn't consider herself sexy and gorgeous, then I didn't either. Because of that, sex soon became an issue. Of course, for her, this was the perfect confirmation of her low self-esteem – everything she had ever believed about herself was true – I didn't want to have sex with her because I no longer found her sexy.

After that break up, it struck me as particularly odd that men are constantly bracketed as the gender for whom looks are everything – but when it comes to the crunch, it appears to me that women care a whole load more about how they look than men actually do. I mean, sure, I wish I had a bigger cock and a six-pack, but really I couldn't give too much of a shit. I think most men are the same – as long as everything is working then hey, it's all good.

At least Candy went some way to reaffirming my faith in girls of all shapes and sizes. She was one of those rare creatures who suffered no such shortfalls in confidence about her own sexuality and physical appearance, and that was what I really liked and respected about her. Many people may think there is something inherently fucked up about someone who is probably three or four times the average body weight. I would be inclined to agree. Opposing that is the fact that for some reason I instantly tend to side with life's outsiders, and Candy was certainly different from most of us. And she seemed to have no negative issues with how she looked – instead she positively revelled in her uniqueness, her weight, her astonishing size. And for me, that was... well, that was pretty sexy.

After a quick interview, we stripped down to our underwear for a photo shoot organised by her boyfriend. I lay down on the bed and when Candy sat on top of me, I was literally engulfed by her body. So loose and flabby was she that mounds of flesh folded themselves around me like the tentacles of a hungry octopus. But, strangely, this was not an unpleasant experience. In fact, I quite liked it. If I have ever remotely felt like I was back in the womb, then that was my moment... surrounded by female flesh and unable to move through the sheer force of weight upon me. And yet it was a comforting feeling, helped by the fact that Candy had retained the glint in her eye and was now pushing her breasts slowly down towards me. And what breasts! I have always considered myself a pretty good judge of bra size, but this was an immense task. Candy's were off the scale. Do they do a J cup? If so then, hers were swimming around in that kind of arena.

In my short time with her, I knew that my perception of what was sexy and what was not had changed forever. It crystallised what was later shown to me even more graphically on a trip to South Africa – that sex and sexiness sometimes has fuck all to do with the physical body. It's all in the head.

chapter 19
the peg and the prostate

Despite having insisted to all the directors of *Sin Cities* that I never wanted anything to come anywhere near my arse, South Africa was yet another place where this particular rule was violated. The place was a renowned brothel in Johannesburg where we arrived in order to make history. A search on the Internet had revealed someone claiming to hold the world record for having the highest number of clothes pegs attached to his scrotum. Our target was a notable 98. We reckoned that with my rapidly escalating pain threshold, coupled with the dextrous skills of a practised dominatrix, we could make it to three figures and into the *Guinness Book of World Records*.

Truly, sometimes *Sin Cities* did take me to a world that I never even knew existed. I mean, if someone had told me when I was a teenager that my future job would involve getting vast numbers of clothes pegs attached to my bollocks for the purposes of television entertainment,

I would have classed them as clinically insane. And yet, somehow, it had indeed come to this. I mean, can you imagine what my mum and dad would have thought if they could have known what I was doing? And what about my grandparents?! Let's imagine the conversation with my granddad at Christmas for a moment...

Pop: So how has work been going then, Ashley?

Me: Yeah, pretty good thanks. How are you?

Pop: Well, the hearing's starting to fade a little, but me and the missus are struggling along. So your father tells me you went to South Africa, how was that?

Me: Er... interesting, yeah... very nice place.

Pop: So what were you filming out there?

Me: Oh... just... stuff.

Pop: What kind of stuff?

Me: Well... erm... getting a shit load of clothes pegs attached to my bollocks while strapped upside down on a large wooden cross, you know. The usual.

Pop: I say, what an extraordinary occupation you have.

Me: Too fucking right.

Through the years I have somehow managed to avoid much chat with close family about my working life. Certainly my grandparents have never had much of a Scooby Doo about what I've been getting up to. They know I work in television, but I'm not quite sure if they realise the extent of my debauched vocation... and bearing in mind they're in their nineties, it's definitely not something they need to be confronted with. My brother and sister have seen bits and pieces of the shows. I think my brother – a farmer – thinks its pretty harmless entertainment. My sister, who is a couple of years older than me, is a bit more circumspect, but on the whole I think she finds it quite amusing. My parents? Well, that's a slightly different matter. Luckily for me, Mum and Dad never had cable television. I suppose I was always fairly honest about what I was getting up to, but not completely upfront. I reckon I probably toned down the truth by about 40 percent in order to make it more palatable to them. For good reason: my parents had always been a lovely, sweet couple who played out fairly protected, solid middle-class lives. Their world was one of conventional, friendly, local village life – think bowling greens, the occasional dinner party, gardening. Not, repeat *not*, a world of porn flicks, cum shots and S&M. Well, not as far as I know anyway.

I remember after the first series of *Sin Cities*, they asked if they could see one of the completed programmes. I was a bit wary about this, but decided to show them the second half of the Melbourne programme – including the nude Olympics (but with me sporting a small G-string) and The Correction Centre (me getting beaten black and blue by various scantily-clad dominatrixes). The programme finished with me being buried alive outside in the back garden with a large snake wrapped around my neck. It was pretty heavy viewing but I was reasonably confident my parents could handle it. We all sat down in the living room for a viewing and I looked at my Mum to see how she was reacting to it. She looked a little pale and upset. My dad was watching with what I can only describe as a disappointed smile. Ten minutes later, and the ordeal was over.

My Mum turned to me, 'Are you alright Ashley?'

That's when you know your mum's your mum and that she loves you. It was a question that, on the surface, showed a basic concern about whether I was physically sound after taking so much pain and torture. But I think she was also asking me in a roundabout way how I was coping mentally with putting myself through such activities.

Well, as far as my 'Clothes Pegs on Bollocks' world record attempt was going, you could say I was coping fairly well. Indeed, back in South Africa I was fastened to a huge wooden cross with my legs splayed and arms outstretched. Then the pegs began to be attached and before long we had reached the half century. The only problem was at that point there was very little skin to spare, but this was just a minor setback. Our cunning Mistress proceeded to rotate the wheel, leaving me hanging upside down with all the blood rushing to my head. More importantly, it allowed her another angle of attack. Although I was starting to feel very dizzy, we were near the point of triumph: 96, 97, 98... Come on! 99! Yeah! 100! Get in! Then I was swivelled back round and just for good luck had a peg number 101 attached to the end of my knob. Back of the net! We came, we saw, we conquered. Well, we had come, but not in any sexual sense. Indeed, much as this had been an exciting encounter, I rued aloud the fact that the charming Mistress had failed to give me a hard on. For her, that was an immediate affront. She instantly claimed that her hand-jobs were renowned and that she could make me come in a matter of seconds. I couldn't let that one pass and decided to lay down the gauntlet.

'I'll give you ten minutes and bet you can't make me cum.'

'Done.'

It was game on. The dominatrix released me from the cross and took off the record-breaking clothes pegs and then began, for want of a gentler phrase, to wank me off. As we hit the half-way mark I could sense some frustration creeping into her technique. The more she tugged, the more I resolved not to let her succeed, and before long my failure to cum had won me my second triumph of the day.

Still, a part of me remained a bit frustrated that gratification had yet again eluded me, despite experiencing the close attentions of a renowned sexual practitioner. No worries, Aidan assured me, there was something else I had been invited to sample in this house of disrepute – a prostate massage. The crew and I retired outside for a quick fag break as Aidan explained that a different girl would be carrying out this delicate operation. The idea of having a prostate massage initially repelled me – the prostate is situated somewhere in the arse, an area I had no interest in exploring further. But I was also intrigued – I had heard stories from friends that it gave you an amazing orgasm, and that for me was enough to tip the balance: count me in.

My enthusiasm for reaching orgasm evaporated very quickly, however. In fact, it disappeared the instant I met my prospective anal examiner, who we shall call Martha. I don't want to sound unkind here but I probably will: Martha was a bit of a rough old bird with dry skin, dyed black hair and spindly gnarled fingers – nothing, unfortunately, that I found remotely attractive. Just my luck! I may be a bit fussy, but if a woman is going to have her fingers up my arse, I want her to be good-looking. Oh, bollocks to it, Ash, just get in the shower, dry yourself off and lie down on the table.

Despite being convinced that I was going to severely struggle to hit the heights of sexual arousal, I found to my surprise that I managed to get a stiffy within seconds. Credit where credit's due, Martha was proving unexpectedly adept at her work. As she caressed my cock with one hand, with her other she foraged around and generally gave my back passage the time of its life.

Perhaps sensing my trepidation at yet another rear-end assault, she was careful to adopt a cautious approach. Instead of pushing or shoving, Martha went for a gentle fingering and the occasional nudge. Hell and arse fire, it was amazing. 'Normally, I must pay for this' sprung to mind. Martha then asked me if I'd ever had my cock measured. Before I could respond she was brandishing an old wooden ruler and pressing it up against my knob end. I had a feeling it could turn embarrassing.

'OK, Ashley,' she began. 'Your penis measures...'

'Wow!' I interrupted. 'Eight and a half inches exactly! Impressive stuff! Cheers for that Martha.' Moving swiftly on...

'No... six... hang on... hmmm... about six and half inches.'

Well, all things considered, I was actually fairly happy about that – I'd been expecting six inches straight. To actually nudge a full half inch over that benchmark was an unexpected surprise. As I'm writing this, I'm thinking to myself how matter of fact I'm making this all sound. But let's be clear about this – I am very aware of how off the beaten track this is. I mean, let's face it, if I'd become a lawyer or architect, my work environment would have been somewhat different. In fact, there were some moments while presenting *Sin Cities* when I'd stand back from the situation and think 'This is utterly fucking bizarre! What the fuck am I doing here? This is mental! It's... it's... it's fucking deranged!' And this, this was undoubtedly one of those moments. Another thing to remember is that none of this happened in private. There was Aidan, a lovely lad, same age as me, who was my director but also doubled up as cameraman; and Kate, a sweet and slightly conservative girl who was assistant producer and also wielded a second camera. And there's me, laid out naked, getting a hand job from a complete

241

stranger who was also doubling up as an anal investigator. Truly folks, this was a master class in multi-tasking.

Anyway, it is fucking bizarre having all sorts of intimate things happening to you whilst on camera, with an audience, and knowing it's going to be broadcast. In this instance it was also especially weird getting wanked off while having my hoop violated in front of Kate, who up until getting her job on *Sin Cities*, had enjoyed a fairly sober existence. She tried hard not to look completely embarrassed, but failed miserably. And with slightly blushed cheeks, she filmed the close-ups while framing out the main focus of the action – namely one gloved hand stroking my cock, and another lubing up a small glass dildo in preparation for imminent entry.

So there were four of us in that room... five if you include the little chap standing to attention. My masseuse was, up until that point, doing a great job. No complaints whatsoever. Considering that this was my second hand-job of the day, I was determined that this one would finish with a happy ending. Another no-show would have left us all a bit deflated: I had my eyes on the prize and things were looking good. Unfortunately for me, however, my eyes were also starting to veer more frequently towards Martha who, let it be stressed again, was no sight for sore eyes – rather, she made my sight sore – and before long, I was starting to think that this was going to be a bridge too far. A few more minutes of exertion and all uncertainty had disappeared... I now had one complaint. A major one. My lack of attraction for Martha was going to be the death knell for this particular orgasm. Indeed, within seconds of doubts entering my mind, my stiffy completely disappeared and Martha was left looking down at the rather sorry sight of one very limp and forlorn-looking penis.

'Oh balls, sorry Martha, it's just not happening,' I said.

There was no debate to be had. No matter what Martha tried, there was little response. Despite all her best efforts, the addition of baby oil and various changes of gear and stroking speeds, she just couldn't get any blood back in the old vein. Worse was that by now, Aidan and Kate were revelling in and openly giggling at my obvious frustration. Martha, meanwhile, continued swimming against the tide, desperately trying to resuscitate my little fella but sadly failing to make any headway – there were few, if any, signs of life.

'Oh, fuck it man! This is not working, is it?' I just wanted her to stop at that point. I'd flatlined. It wasn't my fault.

Martha looked down at me. God, she was a bit rank. 'Don't worry, just relax. Now here's what I want you to do…'

What's this? Martha had a game plan?

'OK,' she instructed. 'I want you to close your eyes for a few seconds and just think of your perfect fantasy.'

Done. I had absolutely no idea what would suddenly flash into my mind – I'm not big on fantasies. Fuck it though, it was worth a try. I shut my eyes and thought for a moment. And then… Holy fuck-a-doodle-do!! In just seconds, I had a full-on raging stiffy. It was amazing: nothing in my circumstances had changed – I still had a girl who I didn't in the least bit fancy with her hand around my dick. Kate was still blushing, and Aidan was still grinning away trying not to shake his camera. But Martha had, in a single, significant moment, showed me that sex is not about who is fondling your cock. It's not about where you are or who you're with. Sex, being turned on, getting your rocks off, whatever you want to call it, is all about what's going on in your head. That may seem obvious for some of you – of course we all have fantasies. We all think of things when we're knocking one out (or in), but to have it demonstrated so perfectly and so powerfully was a genuinely momentous shift from how I'd always previously thought about sex. Up until then I'd always thought that a decent pair of knockers and a fancy pair of stilettos were more liable to get me off than my own brain power, but Martha had successfully disproved that in one fell swoop.

So what was my fantasy that had led to the miracle of my resurrection? The truth, and nothing but the truth is this: I had pictured myself back in England, lying in bed in my flat with the dirty one out of Girls Aloud sucking me off, with an intravenous drip in my arm pumping in pure, cold lager. So how d'you like them apples?

chapter 20
bedroom secrets

After all you've read here, not least my 'intravenous drip fantasy', I imagine you may now be thinking 'Jesus, this Ashley guy sounds well fucked up.' I do sometimes wonder whether what I've seen and done has screwed me up a bit. It's a question I never really wanted to address until now, and the biggie is... how have my experiences affected me and have they left me wanton and dysfunctional?

I reckon the short answer is yes, probably. But it's more complicated than a single, one-word answer, and I don't want to dismiss myself as a casualty. However, I do think it's fair to say I am probably one of the walking wounded: when you have immersed yourself in such a sexually depraved world to the extent that I have, coupled with the added ingredients of large doses of drugs and alcohol, there's bound to be some fall-out. In some way, I'm damaged goods. I'm always well aware, for instance, that I struggle to cope when, after long stretches of filming abroad, I end up back on civvy street and having to get back to everyday life in England. The comedown is immense. Within the space of a few hours I've gone from visiting porn shoots and orgies, staying in hotels, and going out on all-night benders in foreign, exciting new places, to sitting in my flat in Brixton watching television with my cat. That usually lasts for all of an hour before I'm tempted to head off out to try and seek the carnage and kicks that are normally delivered to me on a plate when I'm on the road. And naturally, it's a struggle to repeat the same high. So I keep trying and keep trying some more, and before I know it, a few nights out have left me feeling drained and more than slightly depressed.

I think like all obsessive compulsive personalities I get bored far too easily and am completely incapable of doing anything in moderation – I never go out for one pint, I don't see the point – I still drink to get completely twatted. Then, to ease the hangover, I get drunk again and maybe fuck someone I don't really like that much and feel bad about it. The solution, and part of the vicious circle that affects all addicts, is to go out again and make yourself feel better with another drink or another line or another shag. And then, before you know it, you're spiralling out of control. Thankfully, though, those moments are usually pretty rare. These days, I've got a pretty good handle on things – I can't even remember the last time I took drugs. As far as drink goes; well, I don't class myself as an alcoholic – I just have an unhealthy appetite for drink. I love getting leathered and I make no apology for that.

As far as sex is concerned, well, I reckon a psychiatrist would be tempted to diagnose me as having various issues with intimacy, and that probably wouldn't be too wide of the mark. I think basically the proof is in the pudding – as I hit my mid-thirties, I look back on the last decade and can count only one girlfriend for a period of less than a year. That upsets me. I'm no different from most other people: I want to fall in love and have great sex, maybe have a couple of kids and sit on a beach for the rest of my life. But things haven't panned out that way, and when I see just one fairly brief relationship of any real substance in the last ten years, something tells me that's not normal. Then again, I'm pretty happy within myself and how my life has gone, because, when I look back at all the things I've experienced, I struggle to think what 'normal' really is anyway. Is a sexual obsession with rubber balloons normal? What about sensory deprivation? Foot fetish? Or genital trampling? How about muscle worship? Are these things normal? How many people have to be into pony play or mummification or gang bangs in order to have them classed as 'normal'? I mean, Internet porn and a more liberal output on television has made us more aware of those people with particular sexual kinks or fetishes, but they have probably always been amongst us. However much we may wish to dismiss them as freaks or weirdoes and their subversive tendencies as aberrations or accidents, their tastes and desires are as much a valid form of sexual expression as yours or mine.

My life on the road has freed me from the very British mistrust of sexual difference, and liberated me from a fear of the unfamiliar, of the weird and the outlandish. Even something as simple as dressing up in women's clothing was something that in the past I would have treated with suspicion. Not any more: having done it several times on some very memorable nights out across the world, I know it has had a truly energising effect on me. I'm not saying I'm a closet transvestite, but if that's your bag, then I'm with you all the way. In fact, I hope the programmes I've done, and maybe even this book, have helped some of you with perhaps more embarrassing sexual fetishes feel less isolated. And just how niche and specialised are these so-called perversions really – are they just the pursuit of a select few, or do thousands of us just keep them hidden as bedroom secrets because society is not yet ready to embrace them as acceptable? Your kink may make you an outsider, but trust me, you're not a freak or a weirdo: you're just you. Losing sight of 'normal' is not necessarily a bad thing either. I consider myself privileged to have had my sexual imagination opened up to so much.

The people I have met on my travels have, it's fair to say, sometimes pushed the boundaries of decency and taste. I remember one particular young man called Marcello who we met at a swingers' party in Hamburg. Marcello, who spent the entire evening completely naked, persisted in following me and the camera crew around the whole night, cock in hand, masturbating to himself and not uttering a sound, save for the occasional grunt. In another time, in another place, I would have possibly had a quiet word and asked him to show a bit more decorum. But the *Sin Cities* road was, and still is, the road less travelled. Because of that, I was always expecting the unexpected, and learned to accept that the kind of open sexuality illustrated by Marcello was pretty much par for the course. And looking back, I don't think someone like Marcello was necessarily deranged or depraved. He had sexual needs, and in his case, that was, as an exhibition-ist, to wank non-stop in full view of other people. The fact that he had found a safe environment in which to indulge his desires and satisfy his needs can only be a good thing. At least he's not doing it on the tube. Well, I bloody hope he's not.

Most people, if they were to reveal the truth behind

their own sex lives, would shock others, perhaps even their own partners. While we wave a cheery hello to our neighbours as we pass them in the street, we never really know what they're up to in the bedroom, and as long as what they do is consensual, there's no reason to judge them any differently if we did find out. I guess that's the reason why I have always shied away from mocking the sex lives of those people I have met and worked with around the world. Someone, somewhere very near you could be the kinkiest bastard on the planet – and for all you know, that person could be your brother or sister, son or daughter; hell, it could even be your grandmother. But so long as they're not harming anyone and are finding fulfilment and happiness through their filthy perversions, then I'm happy to class them as normal – even if they seek sexual gratification by running around on all fours in the garden pretending to be a dog. Because, let's face it, I'm as likely as anyone to be seen trussed up with a leather collar and lead next to the garden shed gnawing on a bone, cocking a leg against the wall and howling at the moon.

acknowledgements

Big up to Stu and Paul at Tonto Books for having such faith in this project, for introducing me to the delights of Newcastle and for helping me realise a dream.

Special mention goes to Denise, Duncan, Paddy, Neil, Jeff, Cat, John and Luke. In past lives, Darren Bender, Bill Ridley, Charlotte Black, Donna Clark, JoAnne Good, Antonia Hurford-Jones and Kurt Cobain have been godsends. Enormous thanks to Mikey Georgeson AKA Mr Solo for his art and inspiration. Ta very much to Sukhi and Paul for their read-throughs and for constant encouragement. Likewise to my agent Vivienne Clore and everyone at Richard Stone Partnership. Cheers to all those who found the time and gave generously in their testimonials for this book – much appreciated.

Thanks to all the people I worked with – directors, editors, researchers, cameramen – and to all the contributors who made the Sin Cities shows possible. Same goes for Bravo TV – particularly Rebecca, Dave, Natalie and Jakki – and those at Visual Voodoo, Class

Films and Shine. I'd also like to mention Matt Bailey – hi Matt. Particularly large dollops of appreciation go out to Laurien Dutremble and Taylor Wane, Mia London, Mistress Vinyl, Candy Godiva, Lara James, and Jeff Gord for their help and contributions. Special gratitude to my favourite groupie, Adrie Santos, who encouraged me to get my arse in gear and put pen to paper.

Much appreciation for the cover picture goes to the photographer James Stafford and the lovely Kelly. Thanks to Elliot Thomson at Preamptive for the photo design – top job. Likewise to Sunil and the boys at bluwcreative.com for setting up www.thesexreporter.tv where you can see and talk about everything you have just read in this book.

Fond and heartfelt thanks to Mum and Dad for their constant support, sacrifice and ability to turn a blind eye. Sadly, my father died just as I was finishing the final draft of this book. Dad, thanks for everything.

Lastly, thanks to you for buying this book. Tell your friends about it. Please. Unless you thought it was shit, obviously.